THE ITALIAN

Nella Voss-Del Mar

Translated from the Italian by
Alexandra K. Gibson

Foreword by
Gweneth Lilly

ARTHUR H. STOCKWELL LTD.
Elms Court   Ilfracombe   Devon
Established 1898

© *Nella Voss-Del Mar, 2001*
First published in Great Britain, 2001
Published in Italy, 1994, under the title
Diario di un' Ausiliaria (1941–1946)
Published in The Netherlands, 2000, under the title
Italiaanse vrouw, Brits uniform

All rights reserved.
No part of this publication may be reproduced
or transmitted in any form or by any means,
electronic or mechanical, including photocopy,
recording, or any information storage and
retrieval system, without permission
in writing from the copyright holder.

British Library Cataloguing-in-Publication Data.
A catalogue record for this book is available
from the British Library.

ISBN 0 7223 3382-X
Printed in Great Britain by
Arthur H. Stockwell Ltd.
Elms Court   Ilfracombe
Devon

In Memory of Fred

CONTENTS

Foreword — 5

1941 *Recruitment 53521* — 7

1942 *Saint Nella of the Latrines* — 37

1943 *Corporal at Wrexham* — 57

1944 *From an Orderly to a Secretary* — 85

1945 *Return to Italy* — 105

1946 *Fred* — 131

Illustration section set between pp.64–65

FOREWORD

Readers seeking an outline of the chief developments of the Second World War in Europe, 1940-1946, will find them briskly summarized in this book, but from the highly personal and indeed unique point of view of the only Italian woman in the ATS. The picture that emerges may surprise even some who remember that momentous period.

The author herself quotes the somewhat cynical remark (one of a number circulating at that time): 'If you want to get away from the war, join the Army!' When the Port of Liverpool was fighting for survival, its hard-pressed citizens, starved of security, food and sleep, barely suspected that members of the Forces were living in much easier conditions (apart from the appalling sanitation vividly described by Nella) in places not far removed from them like Huyton and Wrexham. But in the days when Britain was engaged in a national call-up of young women, it is obvious that the Army did not know how to deploy them efficiently; domestic chores were the only kind of work for which they could possibly be useful, even if they were well-educated linguists from the Continent. Nella's increasing frustration at the monotony and futility of army life was of course shared by many British men and women. Yet the picture of the British Army that is sketched in the diary is by no means repulsive. It behaved like a strict but benevolent guardian of those girls entrusted to its care. Some of the episodes and characters conjure up the atmosphere of a genteel mid-century girls' boarding school.

One feels that there was much in the military life that appealed to Nella. Active, athletic and enterprising, she adjusted to the conditions more readily than some of her British contemporaries. Though by no means meek as an individual, she was a stickler for discipline, and one notices that her unintentional lapses from the highest standards of conduct 'escaped unpunished'! She made full use of the opportunities for travel, adventure and self-improvement that the Army afforded. It is pleasant to read of the friendship and hospitality she found among civilians in various parts of Britain that the service allowed and encouraged her to explore. The officers whom she presents to us were people of courtesy and understanding, though too often shackled themselves by red tape. (Not all the NCOs left such a favourable impression!)

A delightful aspect of the diary is the comradeship that grew up among the auxiliaries, as early judgements were revised, in-jokes were enjoyed and friendships formed that have stood the test of a long lifetime. Nella could understand and share the self-deprecating irony of the British, but she also conveys clearly the vision of freedom that bound together a group of women of widely differing origins, notably in her account of the early visit to Lancaster Cathedral. She does well to remind us that in those days of near-despair, Britain could inspire a unified, positive response, leading not by virtue of big drums and statesmen's rhetoric but of fair-minded tolerance. The narrative quietly shows how an international European outlook was being forged among these recruits against a background of persecution and tyranny.

Nella's international stance was balanced by the intense love of her native land so often shown in her story. Her book was first published in Italian, and its enlightened patriotism was recognized by the Italian government, which honoured her with the title of *Commendatore della Repubblica Italiana*. It is fitting that the events recorded in the diary should now appear in the language of the country where they were enacted.

The book is particularly successful in evoking the tensions of the long-drawn-out last phase of the war in Europe, when victory seemed within our grasp, yet peace eluded us. The scenes and people that shaped Nella's personal life at this point give a memorable impression of the general sense of release, expansion and rapidly widening horizons. I well remember the amazement with which I learned of the totally unexpected direction that her life had taken in the course of her voyage home!

Nearly sixty years have passed since Nella and I first met in Liverpool University. Her faithful and unpretentious record bridges that great gap of time, reviving memories of the irrepressible vitality of youth, especially when allied with a spirit as eager, enquiring and tenacious as hers.

Gweneth Lilly.

1941
Recruitment 53521

North Wembley – 4th January 1941
A new year has begun and the war, unfortunately, goes on. The Royal Air Force continues to bomb Germany and, alas Italy, whilst the Allied Forces advance in Libya.

Now, however, one can begin to breathe a little easier after the miserable months with the nightmare of the invasion and the continuing, long-drawn-out bombardments. My wish is to be able to do something in this incessant struggle. My existence, monotonous and isolated, weighs me down even more day by day.

At the end of August 1939, I became a refugee in this country, having fled here following the racist campaign in Italy. From the 14th February 1940, I have lived as an au pair in a house with other Italians who also sought refuge. I have made all conceivable attempts to try to find work that is not of a domestic nature, but every time my nationality stands in the way. Suddenly I have begun to feel uncomfortable, but I have managed to set these feelings on one side knowing that this country has opened my eyes to a new world; a world that I had never experienced before; a world that is truly free and completely the opposite to the one in which I grew up. I was convinced then that the totalitarian party was the right one to bring Italy to greatness, to glory...

Fortunately, about two months ago, a glimmer of light appeared through the bleak darkness of my existence; the Minister of War announced the formation of a type of "foreigners' legion" for women. This meant that women between the ages of eighteen and forty-five from all nations could enrol, including 'enemies'. Needless to say, I enquired immediately about enrolment and since then I have anxiously waited for the post every day. In the meantime I have received news from my family in Italy, by way of the Red Cross and friends in Switzerland and Spain. They sent messages to say that all was well. These messages filled me with confidence.

17th February 1941
This morning I finally received a letter from the Ministry of War. 'It will be another negative response,' I thought, with my usual pessimism. I hesitated in opening it. There were only a few sentences, but they were enough to transform me

completely. It didn't seem to be real.....but it was, it was true! My enquiries into enrolment had been accepted, and the following Wednesday I had to present myself for an interview and medical check. I still feel moved and filled with elation. I read over and over the sentences written in the letter, and no, I had not made a mistake. I rushed to tell the family with the news that I am staying; they were very happy for me, and offered me their congratulations.

19th February 1941 – 19:00
Here I am. I have arrived back after spending the afternoon from 13:30 until 16:45 in the recruitment offices that are located in the renowned police headquarters of Scotland Yard. There were many women there who, like me, were waiting to be enrolled, but nevertheless everything took place in an orderly manner. After a very thorough medical examination, it was time for the interview. I conducted myself to the best of my capabilities, mentioning every little detail of my life, including all my studies, to a not-so-young officer, who only partly listened to what I had to say. Her first words were not very encouraging. "You are an Italian," she began. (I have already heard this said hundreds of times before.) "You will have to appreciate that in spite of your motives, at the moment we cannot take responsibility for you, and so your only option will be to become a cook or an orderly, assigned to jobs of a domestic nature." My illusions were shattered, and my face must have dropped noticeably. Seeing this, the officer added, "But it won't be like this forever; in fact after a trial period, depending on your conduct, we shall be able to assess your loyalty, and assign you to another job more in keeping with your qualifications." After saying this, the officer passed me some questionnaire forms, asking me to complete them straight away in the next room, and to return them to her.

As I picked up the pen, I began thinking. 'Become a cook? Me?' I know nothing about cooking and kitchens but the very idea certainly amused me and it seemed a long time since anything had made me smile. No, I knew that I could never become a good cook. What did she actually mean by domestic work? Would it be exhausting? At least my health is very good! With these thoughts whirling through my mind, I set to work on the forms, which asked me about my qualifications, together with other general formalities. It suddenly occurred to me that my actions would result in my working for the Army for at least five years. Would the war last that long? In any case, these thoughts were not going to prevent me from going ahead.

"The deed is done," I said to myself as I handed over the completed questionnaires. What hurdles will there be ahead for me? I do not know exactly, but they do not worry me. In fact, just the opposite. I want to do my best and try to overcome each one of them. I feel so relieved now. Will they accept me? This worries me! When will they let me know?

15th March 1941
Exactly two weeks have passed since my interview; I still have not received any news. The waiting is torture. They do say, "No news is good news." Anyhow why should they not accept me? No! I do not want to think about these things any more. The Ministry of Defence must have had hundreds, if not thousands of applications. It must take so long for them all to be processed. I could even say that after all, fourteen days are nothing, though to me they feel like fourteen centuries. Now that I have already decided that I am going to join the Army, they could not possibly let me down ...

8th April 1941
...and they didn't! At long last! Instead of the letter that I have been waiting for it was a telegram, saying, "Enrolled". It invited me to attend as soon as possible at the offices at the address indicated. Needless to say, I did not hesitate, not even for a minute. How can I ever describe it, that moment in which the same lady who interviewed me looked at me with a smile, saying that I had been accepted? This so simple and ordinary word had never been so sweet-sounding before now. It means so much to me. The world around me seems to have changed. All of my melancholy, as if in a song, has disappeared. I was ecstatic then and still am even now...I am so happy! Happy for what? To go and wash plates or peel potatoes? I should like to have a minute to think and write more, but I have been overwhelmed by a sudden exhaustion, a tiredness different from normal. My emotions had been so overwhelming. I should

like to go to bed and fall instantly asleep, but I just do not have time to do that now. I need to start getting ready to leave. On the eleventh, I have to be in Lancaster for the registration.

9th April 1941
Today I went to the police headquarters where they wrote "Enrolled in the Forces" in red ink across my foreigner's book. First great advantage; farewell unpleasant restrictions!

10th April 1941
This very morning I received a message by way of Spain from my parents. They are well. I take this news to be a good omen!

Today in the House of Commons there was a debate on the exercise. It was the first time that I had heard anything that I was particularly interested in. It has been decided that the Auxiliary Territorial Service, in which I am enrolled, from today has been integrated and, in consequence, it will fall under martial law. This means that it will no longer be under civil authority, but military.

Lancaster – 11th April 1941
My "New Life" began at London's Euston Station this morning, where I met other girls who will be future army companions. It took me no time at all to get to know the others, who were mostly Austrian and German. On the train I began talking to the girl who sat in front of me. Her name was Becky. Even if she had not told me her nationality, it would have been obvious that she was German from her appearance alone; not so young, tall, big, robust, with long blonde hair pulled up into a bun on top of her head. Her grey eyes had a very hard look to them; the real type of "fraulein". Perhaps she had fled from the Nazi persecutions? And yet it had to be like this. Even her voice and conversation topics were very heavy and cold; sinister even.

Whenever it was my turn, I spoke of my family.
"I have not got anybody in Germany" she responded.
"Absolutely nobody?" I insisted.
"Oh yes, but for me nobody exists any more, starting from my own mother. Yes, I hate her. I have given up trying to understand her. I hate her because she has been cruel to me."

These words shocked me and I did not want to hear any more

from her. My idea of a mother, beginning with my own, is so different! I did not dare to try to speak with another girl after that for fear of a repetition of a conversation of that sort, and I got up and walked down the corridor looking at the countryside as we passed by.

At 16:30 we finally reached our destination. A couple of girls dressed in uniform were at the station waiting for our arrival, basically to brief us and keep us in order. We were shown to our "quarters". We had walked little, but some girls were already exhausted from carrying the weight of their own suitcases, so we took it in turns to help them. After a few minutes, we saw in the distance the outline of a huge, grey and dark building encircled by a garden.

"That is our headquarters," exclaimed one of the girls in uniform who was acting as a guide for the group.

What purpose was the building used for originally? A school? A college? My curiosity was satisfied as we drew closer; I heard someone say that it used to be an orphanage. Poor children! Where will they have been taken? Nobody knew.

After the traditional cup of tea, we were taken to the bedrooms, where we were each assigned a bed. Each one of us had her own bed and wardrobe. Not bad at all! Apart from dinner we were free for the rest of the day.

After unpacking my bags, I started to write down the events of today, but there is so much going on around me at the moment, with all the girls settling in, that I am going to have to stop writing. I think that the time has come for me to get to know the girls who are sleeping near to me. Who are they? Alas, I noticed that one of them is Becky!

Lancaster – 12th April 1941
Wake-up call was at seven. After the breakfast in the refectory, where they divided us up into groups of twelve, we were free until lunch time. I had time to have a chat with the other girl who is sleeping in the bed next to mine. Her name is Hellen and she is also German but nothing like as cold as Becky. She has blonde hair and blue eyes, and she smiles most of the time. I began to feel much better! As soon as she knew my nationality, she wanted to give me a nickname, calling me *"Il Duce"*. Our other companions overheard our conversation and began to

chant "*Du-ce, Du-ce*", which brought back some rather unpleasant memories. Only Ilse, a thin little girl, all salt and pepper, showed objection to the name and suggested "*Garibaldi*". Nobody paid any heed to her as all the other voices drowned out her weak little one. It was then my turn, and I named Hellen "Great Dictator" ("*Grande Dittatore*"), because the film with that same title, staring Charlie Chaplin, had a great success in this country.

"And when is our next official meeting to discuss our future plans?" she enquired, trying not to laugh too much.

"I will advise you with a special telegram," I responded, giggling.

Thus, after this exchange of banter, the atmosphere became far more relaxed, something much needed at times like this when we all have to live alongside each other.

Hellen has a friend called Renata, a girl who is completely different. She is very tall and thin, strangely for a German, and her eyes, like her hair, are very dark. Renata's English was so guttural that it made me dislike her from the start. I was surprised to learn that she is married, and that her husband is also in the Forces as a lawyer; one of their children had remained with his grandmother in Germany. What kind of mothers are these Germans?

Shortly after, I had a long conversation with Myriam in the garden. She is not very young, and is short and wears glasses, but she gave me the impression that she had had a good upbringing. I was not mistaken; Myriam is a philosophy graduate. Her wish is to go to live in Palestine.

"There is a lot to do there, and the life is tranquil without the nightmare of persecution. There must be so much happiness there that the rest does not count," she said slowly and with feeling.

I should have liked to carry on talking to her but we were interrupted.

"Myriam, I have been looking for you for a long time," called out one of the girls with the bed next to her. "My name is Gisella," she added turning towards me. "And what's yours? Oh, you are Italian, *Il Duce*, isn't that right?" she continued, opening her enormous mouth. She too was small and fat and had a smirk on her face. Before I could begin asking her anything, she began telling me about her life, in particular all the trivial things, but in a very unpleasant, obnoxious way. What a contrast to Myriam! Obviously she was not looking for Myriam for any important reason, as she carried on talking in this manner, and I soon lost my patience. "Excuse me, but I have to go back to my bedroom," I said, interrupting the conversation. I did well to, as shortly afterwards the lunch bell began to ring.

We filed into two lines, helping ourselves at the entrance to the canteen to our plates and cutlery. We then made our way to the opposite end where there were two waitresses, dressed in white shirts and with white handkerchiefs on their heads, who were giving out the food; it consisted of meat with vegetables and potatoes, and "the pudding", roly-poly made of some indefinite substance.

In the afternoon we had a great deal to do. We were put in lines to go and get our equipment from the warehouse. We were first handed a sack, then were hastily given our uniforms, together with a seemingly endless amount of accessories; from the cutlery and a glazed cup, to the toothbrush; from a bag with needles and thread, to a brush to clean our shoes. Last came the gas masks. At this point our attention was drawn to an enormous sign with the following inscription: *It is the responsibility of each of the recruits to ensure that they claim every article that is listed on the notice that hangs in each of the bedrooms. Once you have left this warehouse you may only return and withdraw further items with payment.* The last sentence had been written in letters a foot high. We obviously must carve it into our memories!

With our very full bags slung on our shoulders, we returned to our bedrooms, where we barely had enough time to put them down when we were ordered to go and see the Commander. He was a captain, about forty years old, with a very slight smile, insufficient to detract from that severe look. He basically repeated what we had already been told in London.

Our bedroom soon began to transform itself into a fitting room of a *Casa di moda*. Some of the girls had put on their shirts to practise tying the knot in their ties. Others tried on their jackets or their trousers. Little Hedy, on the other hand, wanted to try on everything. She undressed like a flash of lightning and pulled on her pullover and white woollen briefs, with another dark orange pair over the top. The elasticated waist was too large and they came down past her knees. She then put on a pair of thick socks that were also dark orange-coloured and began singing a Strauss Waltz, dancing around the room. After this "number" she was rewarded with great applause and she continued with her performance. Three girls, all dressed in a similar way, acted as if they were models.

"Is this the respect that you have for the uniform of His Majesty?" Becky chortled, and suddenly the door opened and in came a corporal, who announced that we were to go to the nurse who was to vaccinate us for typhoid and tetanus. We redressed very quickly and our moment of fun was left behind.

At 17:30, we went to dinner, this time using our own personal utensils and cutlery, with the instructions that after the meal was over, we were to wash these items in a large basin placed near the exit. The menu was simple, but filling; a big sausage meatball, and on the table there was sliced bread together with margarine and marmalade that we could help ourselves to. There were, of course, large quantities of tea; as soon as the two jugs, one of which contained milk, were emptied, they were refilled.

We went back to the bedrooms where we tried on our uniforms and began the task of polishing the buttons. How tiresome it was to have to shine the buttons, but it did not matter. I felt happy and serene.

13th April 1941 — Easter
Our khaki-coloured uniforms cancel out any difference in age, nationality, race and religion. We are all the same dressed in this way, ready for combat. Can we win this war, I wonder, and somehow give the whole world that gift of freedom of thought, of action and trust for which thousands of people in different countries have already sacrificed their lives?

We were to go to the cathedral, but before setting off, we were told that yes, we had to take part in the procession, but then we were not obliged to go and take part in the service. This is true liberty! Because we were given the freedom to choose, we all chose to enter; God is one for all of us! I carried on the rest of the day without avoiding anything.

14th April 1941
Yesterday began my real true life as a member of the military! Wake-up call was at 06:30. It was a real race to be the first into the shower, go to breakfast then come back to the bedrooms, deposit our cups and make our beds. We were then ready to go outside and begin our exercises. The instructing sergeant was definitely the right one for her job. Her voice was like the ticktock of a watch; "Left – Right – Left – Right". Her instructions were trumpet-toned; "Up with those heads" – "Move those arms" – "Keep in line" and they had the desired effects. We are trying to improve ourselves, thereby to be equal to our Army brothers, thousands of kilometres from here, marching on various fronts. Our day finished with a briefing on the military organisation.

In the evening we were given permission to go into town to a dance that had been organised by our "canteens", where they sell everything that might be useful and where you can drink a cup of tea or coffee.

16th April 1941
The usual exercises this morning. Then I was assigned to clean the officers' mess. The work is monotonous, but everybody's morale is still high and we all worked peacefully. The youngest group had been protesting, and tears were shed. Probably they had not realised exactly what it was they were supposed to be doing and they had become somewhat disillusioned.

18th April 1941
The normal routine was interrupted this morning by a distraction that I shall certainly never forget. We received our military booklets and our first wage packets; eleven shillings. This created a more joyful atmosphere.

19th April 1941
War or no war, Saturdays remain the same, and therefore today we have only worked a half day. After the mess, like birds who flee from an opened cage, we all took flight in different directions. As we were close by, I wanted to go to Morecambe.

For the first time since my arrival in this country, almost two years ago now, I have seen the sea once more. It was like an encounter with an old friend. Tears filled my eyes. The people who do not speak or listen to the sea will not be able to understand what this "meeting" meant for me. From my youth the sea has been a friend to play with, giving me the means to carry out my favourite sports; swimming and canoeing. How many hours, how many entire days have I spent standing on the shore simply gazing at the sea? Its wavy motion, the light movements, the crests on the highest waves; they have always been messages repeating themselves in my imagination, bringing forth the inner song of wonderful nature. Today her waves, even though a green colour instead of turquoise, came to tell me that they remembered me as a trustworthy friend, and they greeted me... For the first time I felt nostalgia.

22nd April 1941
Our health still seems to be at the centre of our lives. Today we were vaccinated again.

26th April 1941
The membership procedures enabling us to become soldiers were completed today; each one of us was given a number. Mine is 53521, therefore we still cannot be in a majority, but our children will soon multiply those numbers. A great sponge has been passed over us wiping away our identities. We no longer have a name, only a number. That is for the Forces, but we shall still try to keep our individuality with our own characteristics and personal traits. Every now and then for example, we can hear the voice of Hedy with her subdued sound, softly singing one of the waltzes by Strauss, or we finish work and come into the bedroom to find Pit, her long and agile legs twisting in the air and then folding into the classical stance of a ballerina.

These minor distractions mean that even in these sad times, there is a glimmer of light relief. The sad fact is that the news from the Mediterranean continues to worsen. The Germans have completed the occupation of Greece and have passed into Egypt. We do not make any comments, but obviously we are not very happy; nevertheless we do not worry ourselves unduly as we have a great deal of faith in this country. Just in the last few days somebody reminded us that Great Britain has on many occasions, if not always, lost individual battles apart from the decisive one; the last.

2nd May 1941
Today has been a little different from the norm! New recruits arrived and we, the "elderly", were to help them become accustomed to the place.

4th May 1941
Already we are "elderly" and we know that our training draws to a close. We can now, more or less, march in a united manner as if we were only one person; we know what we must do, and how we should conduct ourselves in the case of an emergency. It is true, though, that we have not been given any instructions specifically on our work, but then who does not know how to wash plates or scrub a floor?

8th May 1941
Finally today, we have been told the name of our new destination: Huyton — near Liverpool — where we shall arrive the day after tomorrow; the tenth. We are all somewhat agitated about the prospect of going to a real camp, to meet our war companions and to work for them...

Huyton — 11th May 1941
The journey was not very long and we travelled from the station in a motor van. On our arrival, a sergeant under the supervision of an officer divided us up into groups of six, and every group was assigned a small hut. The roadway constructed inside this enormous camp passes by scores of these huts on both sides, but only those on the right are for us; those facing us are empty. Who will come to live there? I wonder. Each hut consists of a large room on the ground and first floors, a toilet, shower and — in some of them — even a bath. (Not many people in my native Italy have a bath.)

My roommate is called Dita; she is six years younger than myself and very well behaved for her age. She is small and plump, and her cheeks are like two apples. Her nationality is

Austrian but she has been in England for many years and therefore her English is perfect. Only by paying very close attention to her accent can it be noted that she is not British. Like me she loves nature and for somebody who has never been to Italy, she knows all about its beauties. We soon became friends. Below us, on the ground floor, live Hedy and Renata; whilst Hellen has been located next door.

12th May 1941
Where are all our army companions? They are here because we saw them on our arrival, but they have been located on the far side of the camp. Shall we ever get to see them?

This morning half of our platoon, including myself, was sent to the kitchen to peel the potatoes and carrots...Peel the potatoes and carrots? I had made my wish clear that I never want to become a cook! Close by me I saw Hellen and it took only a glance to enable us to read each other's thoughts on the subject. Luckily, shortly afterwards our officer, a young second lieutenant, came to inspect us, asking each one of us how we were coping. Hellen was asked first and expressed her unhappiness. I was her echo...We were relieved of our duties there.

The following morning we were given a small sheet of paper that contained precise instructions for the work and tasks which we, in turn, together with a second officer, are to carry out each evening; to look around to make sure all the lights are turned off and that there are no risks of fires. We are to begin work at 08:45 and each one of us is to clean three of the huts before starting our other duties. In addition, starting from next Monday, the seventeenth, every morning, before breakfast, we must march for half an hour; that will certainly build up our appetites. With luck we shall be fed nourishing meals of meat or fish, with potatoes and all the rest.

15th May 1941
Today is Saturday. We worked until 12:30 and then in the afternoon we had free leave. Naturally enough, half the group went to Liverpool, which is about ten kilometres from here.

"What do I know about this town?" I asked myself whilst polishing the buttons of my uniform. "Nothing," I answered myself. I racked my brains trying to remember if there was possibly a name, event, or date that Liverpool may be famous for in international history. I could not think of anything in recent events. I already knew that it is a great port but that was all. My instincts led me to think about the things most important to me; the port of Genoa sprang to mind. "There must be a harbour here, certainly, a lighthouse, docks, ships?" — I continued with my mental monologue — "I should certainly like to go to see them; it would make me feel that I am closer to home!" In the meantime all my buttons were gleaming.

On leaving the camp, I found myself on the footpath alongside the great main road. In the centre, in between the grass, I could see tramline tracks. We had already discussed among ourselves the various forms of transport that were available; we have heard that the one most commonly used by the Armed Forces is hitchhiking. Did I want to try it? I hesitated a little, letting the cars pass me by, when there suddenly appeared in the distance a little van that was travelling along with careful speed. "This one is right for me," I said to myself, and without further hesitation, I held out the thumb of my right hand...I could not believe my eyes when I saw the driver pulling up: "Liverpool?" "Yes." He signalled for me to get in. What a relief! I offered him a cigarette and we began chatting straight away. He spoke of the serious bombardment of the city only two nights ago. I could see the consequences as we drew closer. My heart started to beat faster. Will it be the same at Genoa? I did not go and see the port.

18th May 1941
In one of the rooms, I met someone very similar to myself. Her name is Tony. She is the only person who has until now managed to avoid our two types of jobs; in fact she has become a gardener and, because of this, she has now been nicknamed "Tomato". There are no flowers in the camp, but growing in their place are beans and vegetables.

Tony however is a bizarre type, with rich black hair cut in a boy's style; her body is well built; her legs are as rigid as two concrete columns waiting for a sculptor to come and shape them. Her teeth are small as a result of her constant gnawing on chewing gum. She is almost always alone but today, during mess, I heard her mention that she intends to explore the area, and she offered to come with me; even though she is German, I accepted.

We both studied the map with the same precision, I could imagine, as a general would prepare a battle plan of attack. In the end we decided to go to Manchester in the usual manner, hitchhiking.

Everything went marvellously well. In the town we saw the ruins of many buildings. At this stage, they do not really have much effect on me any more.

23rd May 1941
There was a lot of animation today, but nobody was surprised in our platoon that Hellen, *"Il Grande Dittatore"*, was promoted to be our leader. We all agreed; she deserves it. Along with the congratulations we asked her, "What advantages will your stripes bring you?"

"Firstly," she replied with a smile of total satisfaction "an increase in my salary and then..." she hesitated a little before continuing, almost certainly because she did not want to hurt our feelings, "I don't have to sweep and polish the floors any more!"

Who knows, even without a promotion, maybe the day will soon come when we underlings do not have to use the broom and mop any more.

28th May 1941
Another milestone in the life of our platoon; our Commander, a plump captain with grey hair and very blue eyes, active and sharp despite the superfluous kilograms, gathered us together to pass on a message. We have now been officially recognised and given the title of "The First Platoon of Voluntary Allies". He reminded us of our duties, and underlined the fact that we are the first foreigners to be accepted into the British Forces. Our conduct will be the factor that decides whether or not they will accept other auxiliaries.

31st May 1941
Our lives are uncomplicated here, and less interesting than the training itself. We now have more freedom, but not much trust,

and we now know, more or less, what we are permitted to know with regard to "military secrets". Life continues with the precision of a chronometer. The memory of Lancaster, which gave us something new every day, remains pleasant.

We are not too far away from the main road, which has become the centre of all our travels, and even on Saturday and Sunday it is very busy with motor vehicles. It was for this reason that this afternoon I paid a visit to the same office that, a few weeks ago, had impressed me so unfavourably. Now the building seemed to be hospitable, almost cheerful. It is not uncommon for me to come here, and on my arrival I met two of my companions.

1st June 1941
The beginning of the month has no special significance for us in the Auxiliary Territorial Service as we are under military law.

Today is Sunday. Encouraged by my hitchhiking successes, I decided to go on another exploratory excursion. I travelled to Southport, the pearl of the beaches on this part of the coast.

On arrival in Southport, I glanced at the imposing and elegant shops, and then I went for a walk around the vast and delightful gardens, near which, with surprise, I noticed various pools. 'Is it the sea?' I stared at the beach perplexed for a long time; because it was low tide the sea had retreated much further than I had ever known. *(In Italy there is no tide.)* Then very slowly the sea began to reappear as if down yonder, in the distance, there was a fairy performing a miracle. In a few minutes, nothing remained of the immense beach but a mere strip.

7th June 1941
I should point out that our jobs are not so difficult or for that matter so important in the life of the military; today I was given another free day. Freedom and outings, or should I say travels, for sometimes we actually journey about one hundred kilometres, have become inseparably linked for us.

Where should I go this time? I did not have to think for very long. I remembered that I had heard about an Italian family who were living at St Anne's, near to the famous Blackpool beach. Fortunately, I managed to find the address. I got myself ready in a hurry, collecting my gas mask, bandolier, booklet and pocket money. I set out for yet another flight even though — instead of wings — I had to carry all the heavy military equipment.

What a warm greeting these total strangers gave me! How wonderful it was being able to speak Italian again! Only two months have passed since I last spoke my mother tongue but to me it seems so very, very much longer. How sweet-sounding the words are in Italian, as opposed to those in English! In all honesty I had never noticed before, but now every syllable seemed to be a musical note...

It was simply enough to have a conversation, listen to their memories and hopes, and have a meal that was much more welcome than the ones to which I now have become accustomed. Time flew by. They even invited me to return. Will it be possible?

8th June 1941
At long last, today I have seen steamships once again. I went to New Brighton, and had to take the ferryboat across the River Mersey. This was the moment that I have been waiting for and yet I was left greatly disillusioned. It was not as I had expected it to be; it was a really sad sight. Along the banks I could see shapes that looked like enormous, sleeping pachyderms. These giant grey masses were without any signs of life. I could not even distinguish their names. But because of this new image, I thought about their importance and the magnificent service they undertake carrying troops and equipment, of every type, to other parts of the ocean. How many of them have already ended up on the ocean's floor with their entire consignment?

14th June 1941
Great news: The Ministry of War announced today that there would be a change in our denomination. We are no longer "volunteers" but "privates", therefore we shall become ordinary soldiers like our brothers in the Army. The difference between the sexes will disappear; we have arrived at this point too, now that we are "real soldiers"!

When shall we be allowed to carry out the same work? Our

English Army companions have already started what are known as "operational duties", working in the camps that are located in strategic places along the coast; their task is to calculate the position of the enemy aircraft and to direct the movements of the anti-enemy aircraft core. They are in radio contact with the defence aircraft and thereby warn them of potential enemy dangers. I am certain that we shall never be entrusted with the same jobs, but there are many others that are perhaps less "operational" but nevertheless equally important.

All is change in the last few days, even here with us; Lily went back to her civil occupation, that is, she has returned to being a hairdresser; three girls have moved on from the canteens to the stores, and Eliska — a Czechoslovakian — has become a dressmaker.

Other changes are still to be announced. Who will be the lucky ones?

19th June 1941
I am on my way back from my first forty-eight hour leave. Every three months, in fact, we have the right to a seven-day permit, but in the meantime this one is for forty-eight hours. If we decide not to take the forty-eight hour leave at the time when it falls due, it will be added on to our seven-day permits when they are granted.

This time I went to Llandudno in North Wales. This is yet another place filled with evacuees from London; children in particular. I have another Italian friend who lives there. Her husband, like all the other Italian men, has been interned.

Even though it is now summer, after swimming even in the coldest winter months, I did not now feel like going into the sea. What is happening to me?

24th June 1941
Our military lives have been constrained; from today we shall no longer be able to have one whole day free during the week; only a half day. Goodbye long outings!

6th July 1941
The silence of our road has been unexpectedly shattered. This afternoon a new regiment arrived, taking up lodgings opposite

to us. This is a transit camp for the troops who are to embark at Liverpool en route for the Far East. It has grown so large that until now we — assigned to our duties — had not realised that the regiments are getting closer.

Today was totally different from the other days; shouting, whistles and laughter filled the air. In our rooms, when we are surprised by something like this, we lose the freedom that we are used to. The younger members of our platoon are obviously pleased and we soon saw them on the road, making their first contacts...

Old and new songs, military and non-military, are echoing one after the other; and the young people are as carefree as ever, even though at this time it is difficult to realise that there might possibly be someone without any worries.

All Europe has now been mobilised and in the Far East, Japan has penetrated Indo-China.

25th July 1941
In these days, my thoughts have been far away from the Army; my first one-week pass is in sight. However, unlike the English girls in the dormitories, none of us has a house with a family waiting for us here.

My destination? London, of course! On the 27th of this month, the day after tomorrow, I shall be given permission and the train ticket, and my wages, in advance. All that considered, given the fact that I am not in any particular hurry, I have decided to try my luck and start my journey in the usual way, thereby getting to know the centre of the country.

For days now, as soon as I have finished my work and have eaten, I have got down to studying my itinerary. I intend to visit Birmingham, Coventry and Oxford, where I plan to stay overnight because I have an Italian friend who lives there.

4th August 1941
When I got back to the camp last night, I was surprised to hear nothing but silence. Our army companions in the buildings in front of ours had already left. The road has returned once more to its normal tranquillity.

My journey went very well, even though it was interrupted a great many times for me to change my mode of transport. I admired the rich greenness of the hills and valleys; this was one of the first things that struck me when I first arrived in this country from Italy. I only managed to visit the outskirts of Birmingham, but was impressed with Coventry, much more than I am with Liverpool. The centre does not exist any more, but the town has been kept clean and orderly. Poor victims! I only managed to get a brief glance at Oxford and its famous university, although I have promised myself that I will make a return visit when I have more time to spend.

My friend was very pleased to see me again and wanted me to tell her every little detail about how my life in the Army is progressing. I did not want to inconvenience any of my friends, and so I decided to stay in a little hostel, where I had previously stayed for a few months some time ago. The owner is an elderly Scotswoman, who has been keeping all my civilian clothes for me. She treats me like a daughter. She too is very happy that, after wasting so many months, my life has finally taken a positive direction.

The seven days passed in a flash. I ate sumptuous lunches in clubs and canteens set up for the Armed Forces. The metropolis was full; not only of English people and those from the Allied countries, but also of natives of the colonies. It is possible to hear conversations being spoken in many different languages. A real Tower of Babel! The people who were dressed in civilian clothes were by far the minority; they could be counted on the fingers of one hand.

In one of the canteens I met, through others, a Canadian man. We were introduced and we talked about our respective countries, the Army, military life and so forth, over a cup of coffee. As the conversation came to an end, he asked me where I was staying. He obviously did not know his way around the area and asked, "Can I accompany you?"

I had always been against accepting similar offers, but this time, though I do not know why, I accepted.

It was a pleasant evening and I wanted to walk. The distance away from the hostel did not matter. We were not short of topics of conversation and his gentlemanly conduct throughout left me unprepared for what was about to happen. We reached a large shop on the corner of the street of my hostel; I stretched my arm out to bid him good night. Without uttering a word he violently pushed me. I lost my balance and fell to the ground. His intentions became immediately clear. I swiftly pulled myself up and gave him two resounding, very well-deserved slaps. He had not anticipated my quick reaction; it was unexpected and produced the right effect, calming him down in an instant. After telling him exactly what I thought of him, I ran as fast as I could the last few steps that still separated me from the hostel.

I slept very little after that frightening incident, but I am so relieved that nothing more serious happened. It was definitely a bitter lesson for me!

19th August 1941
Our equipment has been updated today and we were issued with our new gas masks. The gas masks that we had previously been given were the type issued to civilians. Now these have been replaced with those used by the Armed Forces. In addition we were given another helmet. We have been told that we must keep our equipment with us at all times. We have been given the necessary instructions on how to use the gas masks and in the future we shall be tested without pre-warning. Is all this really necessary? Would the Germans really risk using this terrible means of extermination?

16th September 1941
As I have previously mentioned, our superior officers are not only concerned with our physical condition but also with our morale. They are trying to do everything possible to make our hours of freedom pleasant. As part of this, they have opened a NAAFI canteen, a commendable organisation that follows the Armed Forces everywhere. The NAAFI provide cigarettes and cakes and all sorts of necessary things that make military life a little more pleasant and enjoyable.

Our canteen is small but welcoming, with little tables and chairs, and green curtains that make such a pleasing change from the usual monotonous khaki colour that we see everywhere. The coffee costs four pence, and is much larger than an expresso! Contrary to its size, it is so weak as to have become proverbial. We drink it all the same saying, "Be careful. You won't be able to sleep after that" or "Tomorrow you might have a heart attack." One can only be jovial in these situations.

17th September 1941
To make a change, I have decided to teach Italian in my free time. The Commander likes my idea very much and after a lapse of years, I have finally taken up my old role as a teacher. The school is very different from the one in Italy! I have fourteen pupils including two sergeants and a sergeant major.

19th September 1941
It was my birthday yesterday, the third one spent in this country. How many more shall I spend here?

This morning our wake-up call was not very congenial; instead of seven o'clock we were awoken unexpectedly at five-thirty. We all knew what this meant; we were to carry out a hypothetical practice exercise of what we should do in the event of an invasion. In a few minutes we were all ready and in line, just as we have practised. The Commander was very complimentary. If our grandparents and great-grandparents could have seen us, they would have realised, probably with horror, that the "weaker sex" is no longer necessarily that!

In the evening there was a small gathering in the room on the ground floor of our house. I was given small but useful gifts; soap, writing paper and ink. Irma, the very small, fat cook, gave me an English dictionary that I am particularly pleased with. For refreshments, I could only offer my guests the sweets that I had specially put on one side for occasions such as this. We drank a toast with orange juice, even though we did not have champagne glasses, to the health of all of us and, above all, to a speedy end to the war.

29th September 1941
This evening there was yet another bombardment of Genoa, and the reports are that it is worse than the last. Have my family survived? What part of the town has been hit? How many victims have they claimed this time? My serenity has been darkened by this great cloud.

3rd October 1941
Last night, Frida called a meeting in her bedroom. There were

twelve of us there. I did not have a clue what it was about. What had happened? What was she about to say? Curiosity made everybody race like hares to her room, where almost all of us had to sit on the floor.

Frida closed the door firmly behind us and having turned to face us with a flash in her normally calm eyes, she asked, "Have you heard the news?"

We all looked at one another. "Are you talking about the wages or our passes?" asked one of the cooks, being materialistic about her job.

"No, none of those things," replied Frida, who was obviously enjoying keeping us in suspense.

"Come on, don't keep us guessing like this," exclaimed Eliska in a pleading tone.

"All right! If you want to know right away; Lottie will be leaving us very soon!"

"Which Lottie?" I asked. "There are two Lotties."

"I'm here," called out Lottie G., quite abruptly.

"I'm sorry, I hadn't seen you."

"What has happened to Lottie L. then?" we asked, almost in a chorus.

"Well, I'm certain that you will be able to guess the reason why, knowing that she will be leaving us very soon."

Yes, we soon understood, even though the news came as a shock. We should not have been quite so surprised; Lottie is no longer a child and she has nothing to be ashamed of.

"Is she really pregnant? How many months have already passed? Who is to blame? When did she realise? Where will she go to?" Tony was the one firing all the questions, like bullets out of a machine gun.

"It is true," said Frida calmly. "The most important thing is that Lottie cannot remember the name of the man responsible! I think that he is one of the men who came to stay in the huts opposite. It is important that he is tracked down. Lottie however is very fortunate as the Commander in Chief has managed to find her a family that will be able to put her up when she leaves the Forces."

"Of all the members of the platoon, she is the last that I would have expected to get into that situation!" exclaimed Luisa, one of the girls lucky enough to get a job in the store. We all agreed.

15th October 1941
Autumn has arrived; the days are already much shorter. The prospect of having to spend the entire winter in this camp is far from pleasant. With the bad weather to come, it will be much harder to break up our monotonous daily routines with outings. We have had two assemblies during the past few days in which we were asked to give our thoughts and suggestions about future activities — especially cultural ones — for our free time. Today was the day of the unveiling of the new library unit and writing room. As yet there are not very many books, but we are expecting that more will be donated as presents to us from both public and private sources.

27th October 1941
What more proof is needed that winter is drawing near? We were issued with our overcoats today. They are very heavy, rigid and square. Hedy, Irma, Luisa — the smaller ones — disappear under their new coats. Eliska will have a lot of work to do to adjust hers! They drown all our femininity, or almost all; in fact the last feminine thing that we have left is our hair, kept hidden under our hats, no longer than two centimetres below our collars.

Hellen, the "Great Dictator", has been given leave and I have the job of standing in for her. This morning, because of this, I only had to clean two houses instead of my usual four. This left me with sufficient time to get changed ready to accompany the duty officer with the routine inspections. Nothing extraordinary, only a little light relief, but then any little change in our jobs is greatly welcomed.

Edinburgh — 8th November 1941
After all my concern, the time has actually passed very quickly! I have now completed the required period of three months necessary for me to qualify for one full week of leave. My wish to travel is greater than ever. There is no pressing reason for me to go to London and so I have decided to pay a visit to Scotland.

I am now here in the capital city of a country that in all honesty I know very little about, and which is so very different from

England. Before I left on my journey, I read as much as I could about Scotland; its history, geography and most importantly the Scottish people and their culture. My first impressions of Edinburgh are good ones. The city is really elegant and regal. Princes Street, Holyrood, the Castle, they are all the jewels of the crown of the famous Queen Mary Stuart.

I took the road that leads up to Pitlochry, a village at the foot of the mountains. I was pleased to meet a man who offered me a lift in his car as far as Killiecrankie. It was near this place that in 1689 an important battle was fought in which Viscount Dundee was killed while commanding a Highland force which successfully defended the Stuart cause against an English army representing the 'usurper' William III.

I spent the night in Perth; I then pushed on as far as Aberdeen, the "Granite City", so called after the stone quarries that surround it. Filled with emotion, I passed the bridge that is reputed to be the most ancient one in Great Britain!

On my return, I crossed the Firth of Forth and threw a penny into the water as I would into the Trevi Fountain. Shall I ever see my reflection in these waters again?

Huyton — 13th November 1941
I arrived back yesterday, very pleased with my week in Scotland.

I had an adventure this time too; the encounter however, was by no means pleasant and it has taught me that even in this country there is a need for vigilance. I have seen something of the east coast and so I thought I would take a look at the west. I arrived at Glasgow in an enormous motor van, and found lodgings in one of the hostels before taking a look around. I was really excited to learn that I could take a trip on a ferryboat on the Firth of Clyde.

Early on Monday morning, I caught a train heading for the village where I was to embark. In my compartment there were an elderly lady and a sailor who fell asleep the moment the train set off. I knew that I had to get off at one of the first stations but I was not exactly certain which one…By the second station I was so impatient that, after hesitating for a few seconds, I grabbed my suitcase and gas mask and left the train. I desperately searched for someone whom I could ask for information; there was nobody. It was only as the train began to draw away from the platform that I saw the stationmaster. I made my way over to him; alas, the station that I needed was the one after this one, and the next train was at midday. I was going to be late and would miss my ferryboat.

"But I must get there. If I don't then I shall miss my ferryboat," I added by way of explanation.

"Must?" questioned the stationmaster with a hint of suspicion in his voice. I only realised later why he was suspicious when I thought over our conversation. "You can get there by taxi, but it will be very expensive," he added.

No, I did not have any intention of catching a taxi. I left the station with tear-filled eyes and then, without thinking about it, I stood on the edge of the road with my thumb up hoping to find a lift. I was lucky; a kind man with a small car offered me a lift and gave me information to assist my travels. "I can take you to another place where you can catch a different ferryboat. This boat takes a shorter route than the other one, but it will still take you over to Bute, the most beautiful island in the area." With those words of consolation, I felt a great relief. Everything went well.

The weather was not perfect but it could have been worse. As soon as I got aboard, the boat set off. I was happier that I had been for a long time. The sea was a little choppy but I was so carried away, admiring the panoramic view, I scarcely noticed. The view could not be taken in with just a glance. Reality merged with fantasy and I felt I was in another world...

Unfortunately, on my arrival at Rothesay, the largest village on the island, I soon fell out of my dreamy state! I noticed that among the people waiting for the arrival of the boat, there were two police officers. I could not think of a reason why they should be there.

To my surprise they headed straight over to me and, without uttering a word, they ushered me into a nearby building. "Will you kindly show us your identification documents, please?" one of them asked me politely.

I did as I was asked though I was very puzzled by the request.

They carefully inspected my documents, and the second officer, who up until now had not spoken, asked me, "What are your reasons for visiting this island?"

"Purely as a tourist," I answered.

"I understand. I am certain that you will want to visit the

ruins of our castle, isn't that right?" he added.

"Of course. Where can I find them?"

"I will gladly show you," he said, and in the traditional way the British police have of being courteous, they escorted me out of the building, one walking on either side of me. We made light conversation, talking about nothing in particular, as they escorted me.

After they had shown me the way I began to ask myself why they had wanted to question me. Evidently, it was the stationmaster who had been suspicious of my motives for wanting to visit the island so urgently. In these present times of war, my foreign accent had alerted him. He must have thought that he had a spy, or something of the kind, in front of him and had informed the police straight away! However, a potentially ugly situation ended well; the police officers were very pleasant and I had their services as guides!

From now on, I will not start a journey without being confident about my itinerary.

On my return from leave, I received a message from my family that had been written in October — some time after the heavy bombardment of Genoa — with the words "All is well". I breathed a great sigh of relief.

20th November 1941

Our training is constantly being perfected; today we received our first lesson in First Aid; obligatory for everybody. This was followed by an optional class as part of our winter programme, taught by one of our sergeants, on how to write shorthand.

Other platoons have begun to follow our lead; we can now say that we form part of a "foreigners' legion"! The Ministry of Defence, it follows, has not forgotten us; we had another test today and were told that it is possible for us to be promoted to the rank of sergeant.

I personally would have preferred to hear that we are to be given more freedom in our particular line of work! Even though the news is not yet official, we know that this has already started to happen within the men's sector.

28th November 1941

For me at least, the lectures and lessons that we have had in the camp have not been of any particular use. To console myself, I have been thinking about studying the English language in more depth. I discovered that the courses provided by the University of Cambridge are still running. I asked for details to be sent to me and they arrived today. Though the lecture programme is broad, it will be based upon Shakespeare and will therefore be too difficult for me (not very encouraging). I have decided to at least try the exams.

Because it will be impossible for me to participate in the course at Cambridge, I went to the relatively modern, sombre buildings belonging to the University of Liverpool, as I had considered the possibility of taking private lessons from one of the tutors. Whilst waiting, I had begun to picture university teachers as being fairly mature, tall, severe, and with a very professional expression. I could hardly believe my eyes therefore when a young, small, very slim, almost transparent lady appeared in front of me, with curly chestnut-coloured hair, bright eyes and a very springy walk.

"Are you really Miss G.L.?" It was difficult for me to believe that anyone so petite, almost like a little bird, could ever be a teacher.

"Yes, I am. How can I help you?"

I had barely said that I was an Italian, when she interrupted.

"Italian? I am very happy to hear it, because I am Welsh, and our two nations have much in common. First and foremost, our mutual love of music."

Her tiny mouth began to trill making a gentle sound. That made my image of her as being a little bird positive.

After a very few minutes we had already agreed on the day and the time.

"As for the fee? I shall think about it later; there isn't any urgency!" And with a very cordial handshake, she led me to the door.

8th December 1941
The "Great Dictator" obviously has the potential to make a junior officer; our superiors have also noticed and have decided to send her on an "aptitude" class for three weeks. She left this morning. I have to work as her substitute this time too, but it does not worry me, as it is for a good cause.

11th December 1941
Our leave permits are the jewels that decorate our military lives; as we return from one leave, we are able to carry on with our lives knowing that the next one will soon come round.

I have just been to Nottingham, to the university where one of my dearest friends has been evacuated, along with her school, from London. I had the honour as a guest to sit at the high table in the massive hall, together with the rector and all the lecturers, during lunch. It was the first time in my life that I found myself in the midst of so much genius!

At the same time that my private life is starting to assume a more interesting and pleasant aspect, the spread of the war continues to grieve me. In the Far East the tragic attack by the Japanese Air Force on the American marine base at Pearl Harbour has, after all, excluded a rapid conclusion to the conflict. Nevertheless I shall not give up my hopes for the future.

25th December 1941 – Christmas
I have many past memories of Christmas Day! Reunions, winter sports, and happiness. Here, however, it has been a quiet day, with all the normal military traditions quite rightly respected. While the majority of the soldiers relaxed, our officers, junior officers and – poor people – the cooks had a great deal to do in the way of preparation. It started this morning at 07:30 when the officers came in to wish us merry Christmas, bringing cups of tea to us in bed; at 13:00 they served lunch, prepared in the traditional way, with turkey and roast potatoes, followed by a flaming Christmas pudding. It was most pleasant for us, just for once, to see the position reversed! I am not certain that all the comments went unnoticed; the witticisms and the jokes from both sides went on for several hours, and in this way the rigid discipline was forgotten.

1942
Saint Nella of the Latrines

3rd January 1942
A new year has begun but, alas, not a new life. My job is still the same. The most sensible thing to do is to look at everything in a philosophical way, pre-arming myself with a good dose of patience. After all, what do I represent in a vast organisation like the Forces? Nothing more than a grain of sand in the desert! Nevertheless, I intend to persevere in my search for a change. "Who lasts wins," says the proverb, and we all know that proverbs are based on a lot of experience. A great advantage here is that, because of the rules of a long-standing and complicated bureaucracy, one always has the right to speak to superiors. I have been to see our Commander who, even after his splendid words of appreciation and encouragement, continues to respond to me in a negative way.

For the time being, the good news from North Africa consoles me. After so many successes, even Bardia is ready to fall.

15th January 1942
Today, my tutor from Liverpool introduced me to L.Z., a university student who was born here; although her parents are Italian immigrants. She is the secretary to an Italian cultural association whose activities are now reduced to a minimum.

We spoke in detail about various topics, and in the end L.Z. added, "Every now and then we hold lectures. Would you like to come and speak at one of them? Any subject will do. The single most important fact is that our members will be able to hear Italian being spoken by an Italian; in these difficult times it will bring immense happiness to our numerous members who are all good friends of Italy."

"But..." I tried to object, adding that I had never spoken at a meeting in my life.

"I do understand. I know what you are trying to say...don't worry, it will not be a problem," she interrupted, adding with a firm handshake, "I shall let you know the date as soon as possible."

I now have a new project to accomplish. The idea, after all, does not bother me. Oh, I will think about it later!

19th January 1942
It has been snowing heavily since yesterday afternoon. The

entire camp has assumed a more pleasant look and is almost cheerful; the only visible khaki colour is that of our uniforms (*all the buildings were covered in snow*)!

Tomorrow, it has been announced, our general, who lives in London, is coming to make an inspection. The minute that we had finished our work, we were all gathered together to march and practise our various exercises, under the watchful eye of the sergeant major.

20th January 1942
This morning, we were woken much earlier than normal and today's programme had been changed; at ten o'clock we began our training in snow softer and thicker than ever...Our feet sank in the fluffy carpet. For a whole hour we were quite relaxed but we noticed that our officer was a little agitated by this time.

"They are all here!" whispered the girl next to me without turning her head.

Some tried to hold their heads up high, others sighed...

Finally, after a few moments, the sergeant major started to walk towards us from the direction of the group of officers with whom she had been talking. Her voice yelled as usual but alas, not to command us as we had imagined. We could not believe her words, "Every one of you is now to return to your regular job. The inspection has been cancelled."

A great disappointment for everybody!

23rd January 1942
This afternoon, the snow was replaced by rain. Our fairy-tale camp is fast disappearing; we are happy however as we are becoming exhausted having to dig the coal out from the open-air store that was blanketed by śnow. Also we were constantly having to relight the fires in our huts. But what a good exercise it was for our lungs, taking it in turns blowing as hard as possible, hoping that the initial slender flame would not go out as it did so often!

4th February 1942
This morning, I received a letter from the Italian Society giving me the date arranged for my talk; it is to be held on the 12th March. I shall have little more than a month therefore to prepare

myself. In the meantime, I began to think how I could describe a tourist route for an English person visiting Italy, starting in the north. I only have a few books at my disposal; I shall not be able to do much more than this.

7th February 1942
Our platoon, that once seemed so united, has begun to disintegrate. Orders have arrived unexpectedly; the first is for Hellen's transfer to the training centre at Lancaster. It is a good sign and we are all happy for her, as she is for herself. Our famous "political meetings" will now come to an end, but yesterday, at the farewell evening, we promised to exchange visits, even though they will have to be unofficial!

The Commander sent for me to inform me that, with regret, he will not be able to let me take the place of the "Great Dictator", as there are not enough places for non-ranking officers. Shortly after this we were all gathered together to meet our new corporal; this time we have been assigned to an English girl; dry with very few words to say for herself. We now have to file out in straight lines!

9th February 1942
The war is tightening its screws. On top of the rationing of food, soap has today been added to the list. We were told immediately because each week, along with our wages, we receive a ticket that enables us to collect a tablet of soap from our canteen. I feel certain that the housewives will participate willingly in this new sacrifice, aware of the trials that the nation is now undergoing.

24th February 1942
Despite everything, the leave permits continue in regular succession, with the precision of a chronometer.

I returned from London last night after making a short journey around the southern part of Britain. It took me down as far as the popular Brighton Beach and then north as far as Cambridge, to enable me to get to know the town where, in a few months' time, I am due to return to sit my exams.

I now understand why Cambridge is so called, situated as it is alongside the River Cam. This area was once thought to be a bridge between eastern and central Britain, and flourished over successive historical periods. The Romans, followed by the Saxons, Danes and then Normans, all in turn occupied Cambridge. It has an air of importance; the almost solemn buildings give an impression of a city unchanged over the ages. Apart from the university itself, which was founded around 1200, there are many other educational establishments and churches. The greatest, St Mary, sounds a special chime every quarter of an hour — this began at the end of the eighteenth century, and it was then copied by the famous "Big Ben" of London, and by many other clocks worldwide.

13th March 1942
Adventures can happen at all times, even in the shape of an accident, and not necessarily as part of a leave.

Last Sunday at 12:30, whilst I was running to catch a tram at Liverpool to return to camp, I literally bumped into an army colleague. Being heavier than myself, he fell over me! Fortunately his glasses did not break and he had only superficial injuries. However, I was quickly taken to a nearby canteen to wait for an ambulance. The ambulance drivers were very efficient and after taking me to the casualty department to be attended to, they drove me back to the camp. I was put straight to bed in our little hospital.

The twelfth is now too close for me to ask for my talk to be postponed and so, because of this, I had to get out of bed yesterday, even though I really did not feel up to it. With one eye bandaged, I made my public appearance, and my audience, even though few in number, were certainly very attentive.

What did they think of my talk? I really do not know because as soon as I had finished, I came back to camp without waiting to listen to any comments.

24th March 1942
This morning, I was surprised to receive a letter from my "sponsor", who asked me for any news and excused himself for not having written sooner. He could not contact me any earlier because he did not have my name or address; his commander had only recently passed them on to him. The letter

contained a request for a complete report regarding his "investment".
I replied immediately.

29th March 1942
Our restrictions are decreasing; we can now become officers. There are those among us who could only dream of such an event! I am certainly not one of these.

11th April 1942
Today is the first anniversary of my entrance into the Forces! As far as work is concerned, I do not feel that I have contributed a great deal, but it has taught me a great deal about life. Probably, for example, I have learnt to have more patience. Apart from this, it has given me the opportunity to start to get to know this country at greater depth and this has meant a lot to me.
We have all had a pay rise of an extra shilling each week; even though this is not very much, everybody is pleased.
As a change from my usual routine job, I have become an attendant. Most of my time was taken up shining buttons. I finished the day preparing and serving the tea. All went well!

28th April 1942
My travels through the country continue. Last month I visited an area where there are lakes; though quite different from the ones that we have at home. This week I went to pay homage to the memory of the famous Shakespeare. I visited the town of his birth; I went to the house in which he was born, the church that contains his remains, and in the evening I went to the theatre where I saw *The Tempest*.
The next day, I journeyed down to a small fishing village in Cornwall. I found lodgings in a house that does not have electricity. Two days spent living the simple life have done me the world of good.

30th April 1942
Here we are at the end of yet another month. The news from several fronts is better. The RAF have begun the great attack that we have all been waiting for, launching thousands of

bombs over the key German cities. If this is not enough, the American Air Force will soon unite with the British. Rommel has begun a great attack in North Africa, but now, the African Corps have fallen into the British traps!

Here in the camp several of us, myself included, have been vaccinated against tetanus and typhoid. As compensation we have each been given forty-eight hours' leave.

31st May 1942
I have not written anything this month, because I have spent all my free time in Liverpool, having lessons and trying to concentrate on my studies. The exams are close; I want to do my best to ensure that all goes well.

19th June 1942
Here I am, back from Cambridge after taking my exams. My school years have long since passed, and, given the fact that these exams were the first that I have taken in another language, I was quite nervous, especially about the oral test. There were about twenty of us altogether; most of them men. There were a couple of Poles, like myself dressed in uniform. I found it quite fascinating, sitting at a desk in such a solemn room.

At the time I thought it all very strange, and as soon as I had finished, I had a very strong feeling that I had failed. Even if I have, I shall not be too upset. The fact that I have been there and participated, even if only for a few hours, as a student in this famous city, was well worth it!

23rd June 1942
I now have my first stripe! I should really be overcome with joy, but only a small part of me is happy; I should have preferred a change of job! I am now tied down to this unit and, even though I probably shall not have to polish the floors any more, but limit myself to watching over my army companions, it is not a great consolation for me!

Congratulations greeted me, the first coming from the officers...

2nd July 1942
Yesterday, for the first time, I was duty petty officer and the

day was longer than ever!

At six o'clock, it was time for me to wake up the entire company, followed by assembly and roll call. It was an ordinary day but, during meal times, (I had eaten mine first in a hurry in the Officers' Mess) I had to accompany the duty officer on an inspection of the canteen. After the evening meal, I was on duty in the company office where each girl has to present herself before midnight to be monitored. I then had to write up my report before, finally, I went to bed!

Being in the office does however have certain advantages; I get to know all the latest news; soon the whole camp will be transferred to Denbigh in North Wales!

4th July 1942

This morning, whilst I was at work, the Commander of our platoon called me in.

"I wonder what he wants?" I asked myself.

I had to go immediately, but certainly not with the brush in my hand! I rushed to my bedroom, took off my apron, grabbed my peaked hat and went...

He was nearby and my curiosity was soon satisfied. "I want to inform you that you have been promoted to Corporal."

"Oh, thank you," I replied in order to say something.

Aware that I had been informed of all that there was for me to know, I bade goodbye and went back to my bedroom to deposit my hat before returning to work.

Gripping the brush, I eventually said to it what I felt, "Is it really true that I am going to leave you forever?"

Shortly after that, I found out that our transfer to Denbigh is to take place in eight days' time.

Denbigh – 9th July 1942

After a three-hour journey sitting in army motor vans with benches in the rear, we arrived here yesterday. We were all content to leave Huyton, but first impressions of this camp are that it is ugly, fenced off as it is with a high barbed-wire barrier. The camp is located in a valley near the remains of an old castle. We really are out in the country this time; therefore we no longer have the advantage of the different forms of transport available to us at Huyton. What a pity!

There are ten large huts, five on each side facing the others. The first two huts, on the left and right, are reserved as offices and a canteen; the next two for our lodgings; the last on the left for our showers; the one on the right for the water closets.

The discovery of the water closets was the real surprise. "If I get a bad tummy in the middle of the night, what am I going to do?" Myriam asked in a worried voice.

"You silly thing," replied Becky, "haven't you seen that there is also one next to each hut?"

We set off for an inspection, in threes and fours. "What a horror!" we exclaimed in a chorus. That's right; it is more primitive, constructed out of a box with the side open, a hole in the top and a bucket in the middle. It goes without saying that that was the only topic of the day!

11th July 1942
Yesterday we still had much to do settle in and it was only this morning that I was informed what my duties actually consist of. I have to supervise the cleaning of the camp! But it is Saturday, therefore I have the weekend off to explore my new base and I do not have to think about work just yet.

While several of the others stayed in the dormitories, we made our first visit to the locality and were quite satisfied; this town has a long history!

12th July 1942
I learnt that we are not far away from the sea, so I went to the nearest beach, Rhyl; a well-known summer holiday centre. Because the weather was fine, I could not resist the temptation and went for a good swim, the first time that I have done so in this country.

How marvellous! The low temperatures did not prevent me from recapturing the emotions, even more intense than those that I have felt in the months gone by, from just looking at the sea.

24th July 1942 – 23:00
My job is anything but pleasant, especially in the early hours when a countrywoman comes along with a horse-drawn cart with a container on the back of it, which she uses to empty the

buckets from the lavatories. You can hardly breathe in the camp! Today I was back on duty as a petty officer, but I have very little to do.

Yesterday I got back after a forty-eight hour leave that I spent with friends I had met thanks to my hitchhiking excursions. I am quite a distance away from everything but now the kilometres do not impress me any more. I need to walk for about ten minutes to reach a main road, but I have become used to doing that, just as I have had to get used to sitting on boxes, emptying bins in enormous trucks.

On my return from leave, I received the long-awaited news from Cambridge. It was better than I had thought; I have passed all my written exams, with a high mark for my Italian translations, but I failed one of the oral exams. I can resit that in a couple of months.

13th August 1942
The days pass by and my job continues in the same monotonous way.

Yesterday there was a thorough inspection of the camp by the senior officers that had come up from London. Fortunately for them, when they arrived, the air was more breathable. If it had not been, they would have had another impression.

At 17:45, as I was getting myself ready to go for a walk after dinner, Becky, who works in the offices, came to me. Her face was different from normal, shining with a strange light.

"What mystery is this, and what is it that she is holding in her right hand behind her back?" I asked myself, quite perplexed.

"Nella," she began, in a solemn way, "I have found out, informally, that the officers are very pleased with the work that you are doing. I think that you deserve some sort of a reward...a halo, therefore I thought that we should sanctify you." Then with a hint of laughter in her voice she added, "Saint Nella of the Latrines, I deliver this to you..."

At first sight of the card that she had in her hand all I could do was to burst into laughter, just like all the other girls who had gathered around my bed and who could not hold back their laughter either. Becky had drawn a picture of me in my work uniform, with a brush in one hand and a bucket in the other into which my tears were falling. Above the halo, in large letters, there was written an inscription and in the corner there was a toilet. To complete the desired effect she had used toilet roll to bind it together.

I found the thought delightful, something that I would never have expected from Becky. She manages to keep her great sense of humour hidden and so when she uses it, it comes as a big surprise. I thanked her in a few words, and shook her hand whilst all of the others gathered around applauding. We all decided to go to celebrate the event in a local hotel where we happily spent the rest of the evening.

21st August 1942
I have heard on several occasions the English girls saying, "If you want to forget about the war, go and enrol in the Forces." At times I do think that this is true. In fact, we get to read newspapers only if we go and buy them ourselves, and the radio in the canteen can never be heard above all the voices and conversations that go on in there.

Still, I try, in one way or another, to keep myself as up to date as I can with all the things that are going on in the world. I have learnt that Brazil has now joined forces with the Allies but, in view of the distance, I do not think that they will have an immediate effect on the operations.

26th August 1942
Today, I have to note a very special event; I have had my first hot bath since leaving Huyton! A Welsh couple who do not have children, and whom I met, as usual, when I was hitchhiking, offered me this wonderful opportunity. They live quite close to the camp and I did not give them a chance to repeat the invitation. I readily accepted their offer and agreed to return again in the future.

This couple are members of the Welsh Nationalist Group, and I wanted to try to find out how far their nationalism went. It was absolutely at a maximum; the taps of the basin in the bathroom have the Welsh initials for "hot" and "cold" etched into them. Newspapers, books, and the radio are all in Welsh; the English language seems as though it does not exist. I consider myself honoured that they made such an exception for me. They are both very kind, and therefore I want to respect their ideas without questioning their motives and without giving opposing ideas.

This brief but wonderful change made me appreciate the value of a house. Is it not true that "the house is the place where we may grumble the most, but it is also the place where we are treated in the best of ways"?

9th September 1942
My first trip to Scotland with its uplands and moors, mountains and lakes, and its most cordial and hospitable people (who are not greedy like people elsewhere in the world), left me with a great desire to return as soon as possible to get to know the country better.

Here I am back from another visit, this one without any incidents like the last time (I had got advance information about trains and ferry). I went as far as the Isle of Skye, in the centre of the Hebrides. I shall never forget the route that I took, travelling by bus, between the point where I disembarked and Portree. It is a road that winds, like the laces in a pair of shoes, around the foot of the magnificent mountains, and then rises up to a shoulder that overlooks the sea. The countryside reminds me of the Ligure Riviera, and while I watched the waves that played and crashed against the rocks, I seemed to hear in the distance the music of Mendelssohn who was inspired by these places.

I would have stayed there for days and days, timelessly, just watching and forgetting about the rest of the world passing by. It was chance that made me put my hand in my pocket...what is that hard thing next to my handkerchief? Alas, my military book with the "pass" for my leave, which had almost come to an end! Reality was calling me back to my duties; I went to catch the return bus in a hurry.

I did have enough time, however, to pay a brief visit to Loch Ness — the lake was so blue that it made me recall my memories of the Mediterranean. On the left bank, in a small white house that I visited, there is a type of paw preserved like a relic, which apparently had belonged to the famous monster of the lake.

Back at the camp there was some news waiting for me; I have been assigned to another job. My vague hopes that it might perhaps be something better than the last one soon vanished! I now have to supervise the cleaning of the canteen and the dormitories as well as the associated services that are located in a garage. It isn't much good, but it will provide me with a change and so I shall accept it without question.

Tomorrow morning I have to begin work at 05:30 but I shall be finished by 14:00!

15th September 1942
My new job does not proceed easily. For the first time, I have all the English girls under me; they are not very complimentary. As soon as they saw me, they expressed their feelings and opposition to having to work under a foreigner. They began their attack well and truly, but I have accepted it without saying anything, so as not to make the situation any worse than it really is. Today however, having been insulted by a very young, blonde girl, I had her called before the officer in charge. I do not think it will make much difference, though. I think that I was better off before I had this stripe.

19th September 1942
Yesterday was my birthday and it coincided with Ann's, a Scottish girl who has just reached twenty-one years of age. Her parents came to visit her for the occasion. We held a big party in our hut; even the Commander came to wish us many happy returns! I received the usual presents that we exchange between our dormitories, but for me the present that I appreciated most was a letter, via Switzerland, containing the happy news from home that all is going well.

2nd October 1942
Since yesterday, we have a little wireless in our hut; we can now keep more up to date with any developments in the military operations.

No change in sight for me! I obtained this news during an interview with an officer who had travelled up from London, and who has special responsibility for the foreigners.

Ever since we arrived at this camp, we have all been asking ourselves if we shall have to spend the winter here; the camp's equipment has not been adapted to face the severities of the winter cold. We are right. It has been confirmed today, in an official announcement, that we shall be transferred from the dormitories before the end of the month. We are all very happy about the move, but where shall we end up this time?

13th October 1942
In the past few days, the regularity and monotony that we are so used to has at last begun to change. The transfer, goodness knows why, has excited everybody much more than the last time. Dances, variety acts, and films have started coming into our camp, the camp of our army brothers and into the community halls, just as if it is a period of special festivity.

Late today, there was a farewell for our Commander, who is being transferred to another company. We are all pleased to see that one of our officers, who had been promoted to the rank of a sublieutenant, is now a captain.

21st October 1942
This afternoon, I had a meeting that was out of the ordinary with a compatriot who is a prisoner of war. I recognised him from a distance by the brown overalls, taking a walk outside the town. The pleasantness of our meeting was however marred by the fact that, as he is a Sicilian, I had difficulty in understanding him. (*In Italy there are several dialects each belonging to different regions with departures from the standard diction.*) He said that he is well, that he has everything that he needs and that he is getting satisfaction from the job he is doing.

24th October 1942
Here at the camp, military life has slowed down a little but action on the front is just the opposite. From our little radio, I have learnt that Genoa has been bombed again for two consecutive nights. It seems that the damages are enormous, and that there have been a large number of victims. I have sent a message to my friends in Switzerland asking for any news about my parents.

29th October 1942
Today, we have been officially informed about our new destination; it is to be a training centre for recruits at Wrexham;

a Welsh town to the southwest of here. General disappointment, especially amongst the younger girls; they feel that there will not be many opportunities to meet with the "stronger sex"!

8th November 1942
We are getting ourselves organised in our new camp. Just the opposite to the previous one, this is enormous, and is divided into two parts; on one side there are the usual huts where we have been installed and, on the other side, there is a real barracks; the home of a very famous Welsh regiment who are now in active service on the front. A few of the men from the regiment have remained here, together with their mascot, a beautiful white goat who grazes peacefully in the fields around the barracks.

Our hut is the same as our others apart from the beds, which are now bunks. My current job is to supervise one of the recruits' messes.

Our lives have been toughened since our arrival here. The discipline is very strict. "You must set an example to the recruits" is what we have been told. In addition to the marches and so forth, we have started to do gymnastics and now are obliged to participate in the briefings, organised by an official from the Ministry of War; this is to keep us up to date with current affairs and both political and military activities. I am pleased about this, because I think that it is necessary that we are kept informed.

12th November 1942
As from yesterday, I have changed jobs. It means that I shall have some simple responsibilities; making, first thing in the morning, a list of any people who do not feel very well and who would like to be examined by a doctor; distributing the post (bringing cheerful greetings!); preparing the documents for leaves; checking any discrepancies and other similar chores. It is not very much but at least it is a clean job, and best of all I can do it on my own!

22nd November 1942
I am not writing these lines in my hut, as usual, but from the camp's small infirmary. I have had flu since yesterday, nothing

serious, and so I am not isolated but share the hospital ward with other bed-bound patients. I do not mind this extra rest in the slightest. Being looked after by a very kind nurse completes this picture.

"Are you happy to be here?" asked the person in the bed on my right, opening her eyes wide with surprise.

"I cannot say that I am happy, but only that I am not unhappy, and that I can confirm."

She looked at me with an air of pity, thinking that my mind must not be quite right.

The only unpleasant thing is that yesterday evening they caught me measuring my own temperature with my thermometer, and they have confiscated it until I get out of here.

24th November 1942
My flu has now gone. I have been discharged from the hospital and given the whole day off.

26th November 1942
Progress in my job seems to be virtually nonexistent, like a shrimp. This morning, in fact, the sergeant major informed me that I must return to my old job of surveying the cleaning of the "Mess"! It is not the nature of the work that bothers me, so much as the association with girls of this type, who are normally so lazy.

29th November 1942
Returning from Liverpool, where I spent the weekend, I arrived back just in time to hear Churchill's speech directed, in particular, at the Italians. Will they hear his warnings?

2nd December 1942
The conduct of the girls under my command is going from bad to worse and today two of them insulted me. Without hesitation, I proceeded to issue a report; the follow-up action of which was a hearing chaired by the Company Commander.

They have each been sentenced to two days of hard work on top of their normal workloads. Unfortunately, however, they have got away lightly, and are not unduly bothered by their punishment!

13th December 1942
Yet another period of leave is over. I went south again, but this time I did not travel around very much. The focal point of my visit was London, where I spent several very concentrated days resitting the exam there, instead of going back to Cambridge.

I also paid a visit to Canterbury and the surrounding area.

In London, I took part in a reunion of the "Free Italy Movement", of which I have been a member for a long time. I had the opportunity to visit the Italian section of the BBC, who asked me to write "something" to be transmitted to the women of Italy. Just as with my talk in Liverpool, I was left dumbfounded but not for very long; the very fact that I am in the Forces gives me a lot of different opportunities. "All right then," I replied, "and when does this 'something' have to be ready?"

"As soon as possible."

The same evening, in the office of a friend, I typed almost a page about the reasons why I chose to enrol as an auxiliary. The following day I finished it off and took it to the BBC. If it gets approval, they will contact me to let me know what day I shall have to go along for the broadcast.

It is comforting to know that, even if the Army does not allow me to contribute as I wish, it does provide me with the opportunity to unfold other interesting activities.

Waiting to hear from the BBC and also from Cambridge, together with longing for news of my parents, is all making me more impatient than ever. With many thoughts running through my mind, I did not give my work much priority. I had only just started work when I was told that there was to be a change! It is not anything that will make a great difference; now I must supervise the cleaning of the canteens.

I have had an interview with our platoon officer and I learnt from her that, before the transmission of anything on radio, I must have authorisation from the Ministry of War.

With luck, it should not take too long to process my request. I have already prepared my application together with a copy of the broadcast in my own handwriting, which I shall submit tomorrow.

26th December 1942
I have now spent my second Christmas in the Forces! The same

as last year, it was a workday for the officers but not for us! We had a similar lunch to last year's, with turkey and a flaming Christmas pudding. In the evening we had a great masquerade ball!

1943
Corporal at Wrexham

5th January 1943
The new year has begun; will it bring the peace that we long for? "New year, new life," says the proverb, but I do not appreciate the newness very much. It involves work again, as usual. I have been relieved of my previous duties regarding the mess and the canteen and now I have to spend my time overseeing the general cleaning of the whole camp. I have six girls under me this time; none of them are enthusiastic about their work and you could say that they have "low energy". The worst thing is that the sergeant major, who is my superior, refuses to compromise! She is a typical spinster and, unfortunately, retains all of her sharpness just for us! She assembled us all together to explain various things, after which she spoke to me; in a few words, she made it quite clear that I have to pretend that "all the girls are in the first rank of discipline".

It was fortunate that she did not see, or hear, the witticisms and comments that her words had given rise to! "Leave her to sing," exclaimed Beryl, a very thin nineteen-year-old girl, all nerves with little femininity.

I realized that I have a difficult time ahead of me!

11th January 1943
My fears are not unfounded; the girls have given me a "good thread to burn", and I was only too pleased to have the weekend off and to spend it with friends.

For the first time, my return journey did not go as smoothly as it might have done. I arrived back in Liverpool too late last night and as a consequence missed the last train. I did not want anyone to think that I am a deserter and had disappeared, and I went straight to the police station.

The policeman on duty was not at all pleased to see me. "Things like this happen every day!" he exclaimed before I had much chance to hand him my documents. He immediately telephoned the camp to alert them to what had happened.

Bad luck, alas, followed me for a while longer; I found myself having to sleep in one of the hostels and I woke up at 05:15 instead of 05:00. This tardiness prevented me from catching the first train.

At that stage, I went to the entrance of the tunnel under the River Mersey and managed to get a lift. By means of two motor vehicles and one bus, I managed to get back to camp just in time to begin work.

The camp, as I have already said, is immense; all I seem to do is to run round the length and breadth of it about ten times a day. I have named our sergeant major "The Vulture" because, cycling around, she bombards me with the invariable question, "Where are the girls?"

At the beginning, the girls made me go round in circles looking for them, but now I know where to find them; near to the long row of toilets which they clean after a fashion (they have already refused to clean them several times saying that they were too dirty, meaning that I had to clean them myself) and in which they lock the door with a key so that they can then smoke in peace.

21st January 1943
Today, I put all my melancholy on one side because I have finally received my long-awaited certificate from Cambridge. I am therefore freed from one of my worries. What a relief!

24th January 1943
Yesterday afternoon, Saturday, I went to Liverpool to celebrate the fact that I have finally got my certificate. The tutor who has helped me with my studies is also very pleased for me, and I bought dinner for her, one of my friends and two of the girls from my dormitory. It was a truly pleasant and cheerful evening, of a kind that has not happened in a long while; a pleasant interval in my miserable military life!

The day ended with some good news; the Allies have taken Tripoli!

5th February 1943
Mussolini has dismissed the entire government because some of the members had suggested that they should make peace with the Allies. Ciano has become the Ambassador for the Vatican and he has himself become the Minister for Foreign Affairs. Why these changes? Are the relations between them no longer good?

8th February 1943
This morning, I had a truly extraordinary offer; to speak to the entire company the day after tomorrow. There are many things that I could talk about, but given the military and political news, I think that I shall talk about Italy's position in this war.

11th February 1943
Even though I was quite nervous — it was the first time that I had spoken to an English public audience — all went well, and I was paid many compliments afterwards!

15th February 1943
I am very happy because I have received, by way of Switzerland, the good news that Renzo, my brother, has married. It means that their lives are continuing fairly normally.

Our city however, unfortunately and inevitably, is continually being bombarded without interruption. Now it is also Milan and La Spezia that are being hit. How much longer will this war carry on?

28th February 1943
Yesterday, I got back from Denbigh where I had been to visit the Welsh couple that had been so kind to me. They were very pleased to see me, and they served me a sumptuous meal and, at the end, gave me a bag with honey and six fresh eggs. A true rarity!

London — 13th March 1943
I have been here since yesterday; I am on another leave. Before I left the camp, I went to the offices to collect my permit and wages. While I was there, I was told that a letter had arrived for me from the Minister of War; it was the authorisation that I needed to speak on the radio. I contacted the BBC, and learnt that they are pleased with what I have written, and they have accepted it. They invited me to return the following Wednesday to record it for the radio.

14th March 1943
Today, an attempt was made to murder Hitler. Unfortunately, it was not successful!

17th March 1943
My script and voice have become eternal...nobody can erase them!

Cowes – 19th March 1943
It has been quite some time since I have seen the sea and I was beginning to feel real nostalgia. I decided to visit the Isle of Wight; I am now at the island's capital. I crossed from Southampton where I had to spend the night. Because it is a major port, I had imagined that it would have undergone damage, but the destruction, sadly, exceeded every expectation!

This morning at 08:00, I was already aboard the ferry, and the anchor was soon raised. What a pleasure it was to hear the waves lashing against the boat! The moment that I disembarked, I decided to go around the island. I found a farm where they made me welcome, and I had an excellent meal.

On my return to Cowes, I went into a bar that was full of fishermen from different countries; mostly French. I was the only woman there, but my presence did not create any unpleasant comments. The atmosphere was very happy; in one corner there was a small group who were singing; another, nearby, were playing dice. It was as though it was one very large family. What a difference from the typical English bar!

Wrexham – 22nd March 1943
I was so sad yesterday to have to make my return journey to this camp! What has happened to the happiness, the singing and the cordiality that I was able to find in those few days? Perhaps it was all just a dream? No, fortunately, it was not a dream, and the fact of being able to return in thought to those pleasant moments makes me better able to overcome the present monotony and depression. As the chances of a change of job here are seemingly impossible, they have advised me to ask for a transfer, and so this morning I went to the Commander's office. I learnt that it would not be as easy as I had hoped; there is only one vacant place for a noncommissioned officer.

"If it is like that then, I shall gladly renounce my stripes, voluntarily," I said without hesitating, "and I will put it into writing immediately."

Who knows why the Commander did not want me to do that and sent me away! How much longer do I have to remain here?

28th March 1943
I changed my lodging yesterday. I am now in one of the buildings of the male regiment and, with twenty-three other girls, I am in a dormitory with nine beds. These girls seem to me nicer and more ladylike than the others. I feel a little better! Unfortunately, however, the sergeant major pounced on me again and attacked me for being five minutes late at the start of work. Shortly afterwards, for another similar misdemeanour, she threatened to put me on report!

I suddenly imagined the charge..."for having been five minutes late in starting the execution of her most high and delicate chores; for not having cleaned a toilet thoroughly and for omitting to collect little scraps of paper flying in some corner of the camp..."

29th March 1943
Today, I was expecting to listen to my talk on the radio and, with a few roommates, had gone into a dormitory with the wireless set; at the moment in question, there was another programme on in its place. What a disappointment! What could have happened? I wrote to the BBC at once to ask them for an explanation.

31st March 1943
By now, I know the girls working for me well enough not be shocked by their words or their actions, but what happened to me today went too far! At 10:30, as usual, we began our half-hour break during which we take it easy by having a cup of coffee, reading the newspaper or the post, and if there is anyone about, by having a chat. At 11:00, I went to look for my "little sheep" to see if they had started back to work, and I realized that one of them was missing. None of the others had seen her, and all of our searches of the camp were in vain. She is a small blonde girl, very polite but, unfortunately, her legs are bowed to the point where I still cannot believe how she was accepted into the Forces. Fortunately the sergeant major was nowhere to

be seen and so at lunch time I carried on searching…nothing!

At 14:00 I caught her running. "Where did you get to this morning?" I asked her.

"I got married," she exclaimed, using the same tone of voice that you would use to say, "I have bought a pair of shoes," or something of the sort! Raising her left hand, she added, "Look at my ring!"

For a while I was speechless, then, as though I did not quite grasp what she had said, I asked, "You got married? Who to? And why did you not say anything to me before?" To tell the truth, I was thinking more about my own position than about her marriage. "Do you realise that you have put me into a very awkward situation? Naturally I have to make a report of this; you deserted the Army for three and a half hours."

She was probably expecting to hear this news, as she did not seem too distressed at the fact. "My husband is a sergeant…oh, I am so happy! What chores do I have to do?"

I sent her to wash that happiness off her face, working amongst the rubbish bags that have to be ready to be taken away at 16:00.

2nd April 1943
Betty, the young blonde girl who had married in secret, was told her punishment this morning. She has got away quite lightly; on top of her normal work duties, she has to do some extra heavy work for four days.

The Controller of the BBC has at last been in contact. I learnt that, at the last minute, the programme schedule had to undergo a change and so my broadcast went on air an hour before the allotted time. I hope that it has been recorded, so that I shall have the opportunity to hear it another time.

9th April 1943
I handed over yet another request to the Commander for a transfer. Seeing my desperation, he suggested that I should talk to the officer in charge of the exams for the selection and classification of the recruits.

I did not give him the chance to repeat the offer; I sat a test that I did not find at all difficult. What will the results be?

Fred as a child

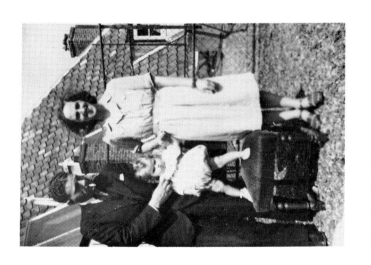

Fred and Nella, with daughter Vivian

Lucca, April 1946

'In our club' — Venice, October 1946

Naples, 1946

Saint Nella of the Latrines, drawn by Becky

'Cleaning Uniform' — Huyton, 1941–42

'Il Duce' and the 'Great Dictator' (Hellen) — Huyton 1942

Huyton, 1941–42

September 1943

In the last few days, the British Air Force has bombed, day and night, Kiel, Essen, Paris and Anversa, causing great damage.

12th April 1943
This morning the Commander sent for me and I was told that I had passed all the tests. I asked him if I could now be sent on a secretarial course. Can I get a positive response for once? Oh, no!
"There are no vacancies," was the reply.

17th April 1943
As it is Saturday, to try to forget the disappointment, I went to spend the afternoon at Chester. I went rowing on the Dee, the river that runs through the city, together with some nurses from New Zealand whom I had met some time ago. It reminded me of the times that I had spent rowing early in the mornings at Genoa. How happy I had felt in those times!

23rd April 1943
My cultural activities continue. The captain who commands the men's military group (I have only seen him a couple of times) came to ask me to write an article for a new weekly that will shortly start to be published for the camp. I do not know how he got to know about my writing; probably from the Commander. I replied that I would do it, gladly. But on what? I shall have to give it some thought.
 I received a letter from the BBC; it was the payment for my broadcast. The sum was much higher than I had imagined; four guineas for four and a half minutes! Here it is, a way to get rich quickly, but it really is not quite my cup of tea! Naturally, however, I am very pleased.

28th April 1943
Another big surprise arrived in the post for me; a letter from someone called Malcolm. As I do not know anyone by that name, I double-checked the address to make certain that it was not a mistake. No, it was not; therefore I began to read the letter and soon solved the mystery. Malcolm is a soldier from the Eighth Army working in an office in Alexandria in Egypt. He met my aunt and my cousins and they offered him hospitality

and, in return, he offered to send their news on to me. It arrived here this way much faster than if they had sent a letter themselves. I am happy to learn that all is well and, in particular, that they had heard my broadcast.

7th May 1943
The English have entered Tunisia and the Americans, Biserta!

12th May 1943
The first chapter of the book of this war has been completed. The last group of the mighty Afrika Corps, one hundred thousand men, have surrendered to the Allies. We are all delighted, because there is no doubt now about the final victory. It is only a question of time.

15th May 1943
The joy about the good military news does not seem to have had any effect upon our officers.

Today, "for a change", I was called the "little coffee bean" again by someone who works in the stores and the camp in general. Unlike her colleagues, she uses some very offensive words that really have hurt me. I immediately went to the Commander and asked her to take my stripe back and to change my job. She obviously does not understood the way that I feel or, perhaps, she chose not to understand and, as an alternative, she offered me the option to go back in the ranks in the mess where I had worked as corporal!

I really am exasperated...but there is nothing I can do...I have, nevertheless, written a letter to an officer to whom I have already spoken on different occasions about my situation and who has promised to help me. Now the officer is in London, which is probably even better for me, because there she will be able to reach the highest-ranking captains. Perhaps it might not make the slightest difference, but at least I have managed to give a little vent to my feelings!

16th May 1943
Today the Lido of Rome has been bombed, two days after Palermo and Civitavecchia. Are these raids the prelude to an offensive on Italian territory? I do hope so!

All members of the first platoon have been vaccinated again.

25th May 1943
Our Commander has been transferred and she left yesterday. Without losing any time, I went straight to the lady who has taken her position. She had already been part of our company and therefore was, more or less, knowledgeable about my case.

From her, finally, I learnt that there had been an attempt to give me a job in the educational field (made by whom?) but it had failed, though she could not inform me why. She therefore asked me if I would still be willing to be transferred as a trainee secretary. There was firmness in my voice as I responded, "Yes, Madam." This obviously was a relief to her and I felt a bit calmer myself.

26th May 1943
The news from Italy is on my mind. The large towns in the north of Sicily and in particular the ports, are being heavily bombarded continually. Rome is preparing for a complete evacuation. But what, apart from this, is happening? The personnel from the factories, manufacturing the ammunition, have begun to find out. Without any doubt, this is a good sign for us...

28th May 1943
Leghorn now has been hit by English bombs; they have caused serious damage. Leghorn is the town where Elda, my sister, lives with her family. Will they still be there?

Eyemouth (Scotland) – 12th June 1943
I have come back, with great pleasure, to this generous country. I really do not know how so many jokes are aimed at these people. I am the guest of Ella's parents. Ella is the girl who was with me at Denbigh; I met her parents at her twenty-first birthday party and they immediately offered to let me stay with them in Scotland.

I did not come here directly; first of all I travelled round and visited, not only York with its famous cathedral, but all the other well-known places in this vast county. I even got to see Hellen and after the exchange of laughter following "How are you, dear Dictator?" "Is it you, my beloved Duce?" we began to talk about our lives, and mine in particular.

"Did you not know that since the 31st of May there are no work restrictions for us?" she asked "Now it will not be too difficult to find something better."

"No, I didn't know. You deserve a kiss, but people like us cannot permit such an act of affection," I responded very happily.

"Be assured that I shall take up the struggle with even more courage the moment that I get back to the camp. I shall keep you informed. Goodbye!"

With a firm handshake, we parted.

After Newcastle, where I spent a night, I travelled a short part of my journey by train and then I thought that I would try my luck at hitchhiking. I reached a certain point where I was to branch off and take a minor road in another direction, so reluctantly I had to leave the motorcar that had bought me so far and which was continuing on its way to Edinburgh. So as not to lose too much time waiting for some form of transport to pass by, I decided that I should begin to walk the distance. I knew that there were only three miles separating me from my destination, and I wanted to get there as soon as possible.

After a few minutes, I realized that there was a young man, with a bit of a limp, carrying a military sack on his shoulders, behind me.

After another couple of steps I heard him calling to me, "Please could you tell me if this road leads to...?" And he named a village that I had never heard of before.

"Wait a minute, I'll have a look at my map." Saying that, I pulled my precious map book, with all the maps of Great Britain, out of my bag. "Yes, I have found it; it's a little way beyond Eyemouth, where I'm going to," I added, closing the book.

After introducing ourselves to one another, we began to chat.

Without my asking, he mentioned what had happened to his right leg. "I too was in the Armed Forces, and most recently in the Air Force, but I was injured in a flying accident, and I have been demobilized. I found a good job straight away, but now I am on holiday for a few days."

In this way, chatting generally about more and less important things, we walked the three miles without even realizing it.

When we reached the little town, I soon found the house of my new friends. "Come with me, we'll ask these people for details about where it is you are going," I suggested to him, seeing his hesitation to carry on his way.

The welcome was more than affectionate.

"And this is…" I began, but could not finish.

"Donald."

With typical Scottish friendliness the lady soon said, "Sit yourselves down, make yourselves at home, and I'll go and prepare the tea."

She disappeared, only to return shortly with a teapot and a plate full to the brim with the most appetizing things, and boiled eggs; such a rarity in these times.

The three miles that we had walked had, in all honesty, given us a healthy appetite and so we did not hesitate to take her up on her offer.

Rested and refreshed, I mentioned the name of the place that Donald was heading towards.

"Oh, that village is close to this one, and if you are not too tired, we can go by foot passing along the beach. And you, Nella, loving the sea so much, will enjoy the walk no doubt," explained Mr C.

At this point, Donald bade farewell to the lady and we set off, with me walking between the two men. In a little under an hour we arrived at Donald's village and said goodbye.

When we returned to the house the lady asked me, "Why didn't you tell us that you are engaged? Donald seems to be a very decent boy and I'm happy for you," she continued without giving me the chance to open my mouth.

"Engaged — me? You've made a mistake! I don't know Donald any more than you do yourself!" I managed to explain and I went on to tell her how we met.

"Thank goodness you didn't tell us that sooner," said the lady, bursting out laughing.

In a good mood, but exhausted, I went to bed and fell asleep immediately.

13th June 1943

I got up, having finished a very hearty breakfast brought to me in bed by the lady. Even though the weather does not seem to be too good, I intend putting my bathing costume on, and going to have a swim, if the temperature of the sea will permit me.

Thurso – 19th June 1943
Here I am. I have arrived in this little town that is the northernmost part of Britain! It wrenched my heart having to leave my hosts, but I set off and travelled up to Edinburgh where, after a few hours, I managed to get a train for the north.

At Perth, I learnt by chance that a special military train was due to arrive in a few minutes, and for reasons that were not explained, it was not mentioned in the railway timetable. I thought that I might need to have a special ticket or something, but the train inspector looked at my uniform and let me aboard. With joy I found a compartment where there were some marines. I managed to doze off for the night, and in the morning, joined a queue hoping to be able to go and visit an island again; this time one of the Orkneys. Unfortunately I did not manage to do this, as I soon discovered that access is only permitted to those who are stationed there. I hurried to the officer in charge of the ferry passengers and showed my documents to him, adding that my passion for the sea had led me come so far on this long journey.

"We cannot let you go," he said in a very dry tone.

'If I had been a spy, I probably would have got permission,' I thought in vain. What a bitter disappointment it was for me.

I found out that there was a hostel, and so I headed off to make a reservation for myself for the night.

The warden welcomed me very politely, "Are you really Italian? You don't know how happy I am to meet you."

"Why?"

"I'm engaged to an officer in the Italian marines."

It goes without saying that I was surprised.

I went to have a look around the small town and walked along the beach. The only people who were there were holiday tourists, together with a few seagulls who were taking a rest after travelling who knows how many miles. To complete the scene, a fisherman, with a large pipe in his mouth, was scrutinizing the horizon. As he drew closer, he cordially introduced himself to me. When I told him that I was an Italian, he exclaimed, "Follow me."

I followed him, and fortunately my curiosity was soon

satisfied. We reached the crossroads in the centre of town and the fisherman went into a shop. I naturally followed him.

"This lady is Italian," he announced to the owner, who greeted me with a Tuscan accent.

"I'm from Genova and I'm certain that there is no need for you to say where you're from!" I exclaimed.

"No indeed, I'm from Lucca."

After a pleasant conversation I went back to my hostel to eat. I then thought that I would try to go to John o'Groat's, the most northern point of Great Britain. "There are no regular services and the traffic is minimal, which will make hitchhiking difficult," I was told. Another bitter disappointment, but I did not take it too much to heart.

The next morning I had the beach all to myself again and so I risked venturing into the sea. What a pleasure it was for me, but how cold it was! When I got out of the sea I went for a ten-minute run, making hundreds of seagulls flee from the shore.

Wrexham – 21st June 1943
Having bid farewell, with a touch of sadness, to the fascinating coast of Thurso, I returned directly to camp, having travelled most of the kilometres by train.

I had a big surprise waiting for me on my return. "You've been transferred," said one of my roommates the minute she saw me by way of a greeting. The news really seemed too good to be true, and so I began to read the orders for the day. Yes, it really was true!

23rd June 1943
Waking up yesterday, I had a positive feeling that the wind had finally changed direction and that things were going to change for me.

Alas, my happiness did not last for long! In the afternoon, I was informed that my transfer had been proposed, and soon after that, I learnt indirectly that it had all been a mistake. What a terrible disappointment!

27th June 1943
For the entire weekend, we could breathe the atmosphere of a party at the camp! None of us had been granted permission to

leave; vice versa, the public were allowed to enter. The change was enormous. There was a gymnastics display by the recruits, accompanied by the band playing to bring an end to the demonstration.

5th July 1943
The landing of the troops at Crete, after the occupation of Lampedusa and Linosa, leads me to think that probably there will be a landing in Sicily too.

10th July 1943
My prediction is correct! With great emotion I heard the news today about the landing in Sicily. The moment that I finished work, I was glued to the wireless, and until now (it's 22:30) I have tried to listen to everything that I possibly could to keep me informed on the situation.

11th July 1943
General Eisenhower has arrived in Sicily.

12th July 1943
The Allied troops are advancing rapidly; they are twenty miles inland already.

13th July 1943
These days, I am so excited that I have not given a thought to my own monotonous life, not for even a minute. The advance of the Allied troops in Sicily is making me quiver with anxiety. I only have one regret; that of not being with them! Today, Churchill has announced that women will form part of the "occupation" troops. I now, therefore, have a new and better chance to hope for.

Allied ships have entered the port of Ragusa. New landings have been made near to Catania.

19th July 1943
The Americans have bombed Rome.

20th July 1943
The Italian Army has mutinied!

22nd July 1943
The Allies have now occupied two-thirds of Sicily.

26th July 1943
I do not know exactly what has been happening in Italy. The only thing I do know, but it is enough, is that Mussolini has been arrested and that there is now martial law in Italy. With the end of the Fascist party, another chapter in Italy's story has ended. I think with anguish what may be happening to the people.

The advance of the Allies from the south, the revolt in the centre, new German troops being sent to the north; it all seems to be an incredibly tragic story!

30th July 1943
Rome is considering the Allies' peace terms.

1st August 1943
After the latest turn of events in Italy and Churchill's declaration, I thought that I should go to speak to the Commander. Yesterday, I had a long interview, the main topic of which was my possible transfer to Italy. The Commander showed great understanding and advised me to put my request down in writing. She will send it off for me together with her own comments which, being from a senior officer, should probably help my case.

I wrote the request last night and gave it to her this morning. Will she really write something on my behalf? I am not over-certain!

7th August 1943
Genoa, Milan and Turin have been bombed.

14th August 1943
The news from Italy continues to cause me to have "highs and lows". Whilst I am happy with the progress towards the liberation, the heavy bombardment of the cities is causing me continual pain. I have received a letter from my family dated the 17th July, with the sole message, *"Everything's going well."* But now?

17th August 1943
I have received a letter from Malcolm from Sicily. I do so envy him! I replied straight away, asking him to try to find out if there is anything that he can do to help me go over there and join him.

26th August 1943
The previous news about the possible closure of this horrible camp is correct, and today we received the official announcement. Naturally, I am pleased, even though I realize that I shall be transferred without being able to change jobs. In any case, the change has made me think that perhaps I shall be able to get rid of my sergeant major, and this has cheered me up a lot. Where shall I end up this time?

29th August 1943
I have just returned from Liverpool where I have been staying with friends. I met one of my roommates, and we both went together to the tunnel entrance to try to get a lift.

We were fortunate and got a lift from someone special. We saw an American Military Police jeep arriving. "Nothing for us," I said.

The same moment the passenger, next to the driver, asked, "Are you going to Chester?"

"Yes."

"Get in," he added.

They did not need to repeat the offer. It was the first time that I have been aboard this type of vehicle.

"I hope that whoever sees us does not think that the police have picked up two people!" I exclaimed, trying to break the ice a little.

I had barely announced the fact that I was Italian, when the jeep began to slow down.

"What's wrong? What's happening?" asked my roommate, a little alarmed.

"Oh, nothing serious!" exclaimed the driver, who until now had not opened his mouth. "Are you really Italian?" he asked me in English, but then to my surprise changed to speaking in Italian: "Give me your hand, I'm Sicilian!" he added with a great warmth, "and my name is Pasquale!"

We soon felt like brothers. Instinctively a verse by Dante came to mind, "I am Sordello from your own land."

"It is too late now, but we should see one another again to celebrate our meeting," he said after a few minutes.

The jeep slowed down as we arrived at the houses on the outskirts of Chester, "I am sorry that I cannot take you to the camp. But we are already a few minutes late and we need to get back."

We quickly exchanged names and addresses. We said our goodbyes with a reciprocal *"arrivederci"*, as his jeep had already begun to move off.

3rd September 1943
Today is the fourth anniversary of the beginning of the war; it has been declared "A National Day of Prayer". We went to the cathedral where the Divine Service was more solemn then ever. We said prayers for the end of the war, and for the reunion of our families.

Cardiff – 9th September 1943
Here I am on another leave wandering around like a nomad. I have just arrived in Cardiff after having explored a new part of the country on the borders of Wales. I visited Hereford Cathedral, one of the most famous of its kind, and then crossed the noted Rhondda Valley, between two chains of Welsh mountains.

I am quite tired. I dined in a club, where they accepted me most cordially, and now I have come back to my bedroom in one of the hostels. Apart from feeling tired, perhaps I am also feeling emotional after hearing the news of Italy's surrender, just as I was about to leave the camp yesterday. Whatever will happen now? The thoughts and hopes have begun to turn over and over in my mind, like a windmill...fortunately, however, my bed calls. I would rather trust my mind to dreams because, every night, they take me to the kingdom of illusions and fantasy.

St Ives – 12th September 1943
After visiting many northern places, it seemed only logical that I should start to visit the more southerly ones! With this aim in

mind, I left Cardiff, which, contrary to what I had expected, I found very clean and well planned, and I carried on south.

At Plymouth, stupidly, I made the first error of this kind in my life; I actually got on the wrong train! The damage was not too bad, however, as I only lost a couple of hours getting back to where I had been. Putting all this aside, I managed to get to Newquay in time to find myself the best lodgings.

This morning I went to the beach, now half-deserted, with a comrade from the Air Force. I was very happy to step back into the Atlantic! The temperature here, naturally, is a little warmer than that in the north, and so instead of going for a run after my swim, I was able to lie peacefully down in the sun. I should have liked to remain there all day, but I had already decided to peep into the retreat of many British artists, some of whom have made permanent homes here.

To get here I had to use another new form of transport for me, a taxi; but I only travelled in it for the last few kilometres of my journey. I felt uncomfortable, having the image in my mind of arriving like a lady for an unlimited holiday. The police assisted me in finding lodgings; it is a place where they are accustomed to having guests of a different kind from a simple member of the military like myself!

London – 16th September 1943
Simply by going swimming a few times and for walks, and having a certain good rest, the days that I have spent at St Ives have gone by very quickly. With a certain heartache, I said adieu to the Atlantic, or was it just a simple "Goodbye, see you soon"?

In all honesty, when I am on leave, I try to relax and enjoy it to the best of my ability and therefore do not worry if I do not listen to the radio or read the newspapers. The minute that I arrived back at my old lodgings, I asked the housekeeper if anything important had happened.

"What, you didn't know that Mussolini has been freed by the Germans and transferred to Germany?" she asked me in surprise.

No, I did not know. How could it be possible? Whatever was he going to do now? I promised myself that I would go to buy myself a newspaper to read all the details.

I have been to see some of my Italian friends, all of them

happy and convinced that we shall be able to return to our families very soon. How far away will this "very soon" be?

Wrexham – 21st September 1943
A new ray of light has come to brighten my gloomy military life. I have been told that on the 26th, I shall be going to London with several other junior officers for another series of selection tests. I have been given a completely new uniform for the occasion!

Wrexham – 29th September 1943
My brief visit to London has already come to an end. For three days in a row I have undergone assessments of all sorts. Our poor brains have been subjected to all kinds of tests, of intelligence, imagination and speed. We had to play the part of a sergeant and also that of an ordinary soldier. We had to organise a conference and to use a typewriter. In addition to the mental tests, we were also tested as to our physical abilities and had to do a number of gymnastic activities. At the end of all this, we had to go before a psychiatrist and then we had to undergo interviews with various officers, one of whom asked if I would like to enter the Intelligence Corps. I confirmed my request in both Italian and French. After this I filled in and signed a form in which I declared that I was prepared to go back to being an ordinary soldier.

When I arrived back in Wrexham, I was told that with twenty-nine others, I am to be transferred to Rossett, a camp not too far from here.

Rossett – 30th September 1943
I got up earlier than usual this morning, at 06:30, and went through the normal formalities; an inspection of the equipment, the medical check-up, the pay, etc. All this work for so little money, but in the end, I am content enough because I shall still have the possibility of visiting Liverpool and the surrounding area, to see my friends and acquaintances.

We left the camp; what a sigh of relief I gave it when I opened the gates!

Our new headquarters consist of two groups of private houses. In the largest group are the canteen and the accommodation for the officers, whilst we are to sleep in the others.

On our arrival here, I had the pleasure of meeting some of the girls who were in my old platoon! Soon after our reunion our Commander came in to welcome us, with her best wishes that we should all settle in well. We hope so!

2nd October 1943
The Fifth Army has entered Naples!

5th October 1943
There is very little for us to do here; our main work is to keep our houses clean. For the rest of the time we attend meetings, practise marching, gymnastics, and so forth. Therefore, our lives are simple, but peaceful.

In the afternoon, another group of comrades arrived; included in one of them is Hedy, who is to sleep in my bedroom.

11th October 1943
I have now been in the English Auxiliary Territorial Service for exactly thirty months! After everything that has happened, time has passed quite quickly. How much more remains?

13th October 1943
Some exceptional news that has filled me with joy; Italy has declared war against Germany, and has been recognized by the Allies as cobelligerent. My position has therefore changed too!

18th October 1943
I received the usual message from my parents from Switzerland, and I replied immediately.

21st October 1943
Another piece of exceptional news, but this time it is personal. I received a telegram from Malcolm requesting all my details so that he can attempt to get me transferred to Sicily! My excitement was so great that my roommates, realizing it, asked me what had happened. I am quite a pessimist and, with my run of bad luck, I do not think that I shall ever make it...It will not hurt to try.

This evening, to calm me down a little I went to Wrexham to see a film, "The Red Primrose".

28th October 1943
This is a transit camp and each day there are new arrivals whilst others leave. But today, whom did I see getting off the motor van that had been to the station to collect the new arrivals? I just could not believe my eyes; the great sergeant major! She had such a huge smile on her face when she saw me! Naturally I did not exchange it!

30th October 1943
Whilst in Italy, the Fifth and the Eighth armies are making satisfactory progress, at Naples there has been a conference in which Badoglio, Sforza, Croce and others participated. They have asked for the abdication of the king, and Sforza has proposed a regency.
American "Fortresses" have bombed Genoa for the first time.

8th November 1943
I sent a package to Malcolm today with my best wishes for Christmas and the New Year. What a good man he must be! I received a letter from him yesterday in which he says that he is still trying, together with an officer, to do everything possible to obtain my transfer. He did however warn me that it would not be easy.
Now, more than ever, I can feel how distance, instead of keeping people far apart, draws them together!

10th November 1943
Today, it has been announced that an Allied Commission is to be in control of Italy. How can I help? If only I were down there!

13th November 1943
A temporary administration has been formed in Italy.

23rd November 1943
For better and for worse, the days pass by with the same monotonous regularity; the jobs are fortunately interrupted by

the free leave that provides us with the relaxation that we need to continue to "pull on ahead".

The Allies, in the meantime, yesterday started to bomb Berlin. How will the Germans react?

27th November 1943
My series of excursions continues. Today, when I was ready to leave for the weekend, I was alerted that the officer in charge of the "instructions" section of the Far East Command was waiting for me in our camp.

I gave up my leave, and an hour later I had another one of those long interviews with him. "I shall try to do everything possible to help you, but I cannot promise you anything," were his last words.

3rd December 1943
The Commander called me before him. "I have just received orders inviting you to transfer to work in London, as a corporal."

"I am not at all happy," I commented. "And what were the results of my tests?"

"I don't know, but in London you will have a better opportunity to change jobs."

Yes, the idea of London comforts me a little, not simply because of the chance of new opportunities, but also because I shall be in the capital and close to many friends and acquaintances.

London — 7th December 1943
With much joy, I said my final farewell to Wales! In all honesty, not to the country or to its people, but to all the military camps, known and unknown, and their associated personnel! It did not seem to be quite real for me, but luckily, my large sack removed any doubts.

The journey lasted two hours more than normal because of heavy fog, but the weather was much clearer in London and so I easily found my new residence. I discovered that part of it is also a male selection centre for aspiring officers, similar to the one that I had been sent to, and that our quarters are amongst the finest and most beautiful in London. The main building is a magnificent country house with a garden, almost big enough to be a park, in which, I am told, the aspiring officers have to perform their physical tests. I soon noticed, in fact, ropes attached to the trees, and all kinds of obstacles.

I was greeted most cordially and was pleased to learn that there are only twenty of us, including one sergeant major and two officers.

A few steps away, in another aristocratic-looking, though somewhat smaller, country house, are our lodgings. Next to my bedroom, which I share with another girl, I saw a bedroom with an *en suite* bathroom, and what a bedroom it was! All in light blue with mirrors everywhere.

"I never would have thought that the members of the military could ever possibly lodge in such large, sumptuous houses as these!" I exclaimed.

"The owners of these houses have gone to live somewhere safer and the Ministry of War have requisitioned them," explained Win, my new roommate.

I instantly jumped at the chance to have a bath and I could definitely have fallen asleep in it if someone had not knocked on the door asking me to hurry up.

8th December 1943
This morning I went to see the officer who commands our platoon. She is the most beautiful girl that I have ever seen in uniform. Her eyes are unique, being very deep blue-grey in colour; her voice and her way of talking are fascinating, so much so that instead of telling her my unpleasant story, I should have liked to have asked her questions, and in that way I could have stayed and listened to her. I noticed how young she was, and marvelled to see her holding such an important post at her age; she is in her early twenties I should guess, definitely not any older. She must therefore be at the beginning of her military career.

At the end of our interview she asked me to prepare a written report and to give it to the Commander.

I still have not been given instructions about my job, but I set to work on my report and delivered it in the afternoon.

The Commander, a young woman of about thirty years of age from central Ireland, is also quite attractive but less so than her subordinate. She showed a lot of understanding about my case. "You have been very unlucky," she said, and she told me that she had already been in contact with the colonel from the nearby selection centre; at the news of my arrival here, he was most surprised and has promised to make some immediate enquiries into my case.

It seems, therefore, that the cogwheels that regulate my military life have been put into action. What will the result be?

Here, in the meantime, apart from being the head of the serving girls who work in the kitchen, and those who do the cleaning, I am also the head waitress and have to serve the five officers who sit together in the form of a horseshoe on the central table. I never expected a job like this, but the novelty, and the fact that everything is clean and shiny, have reconciled me to starting it with a good dose of philosophy.

10th December 1943
This morning the Commander, thinking that she was doing me a favour, told me, "All the officers are very satisfied with your performance!"

"I'd rather they weren't!" I exclaimed.

"Don't worry," she continued, "it won't be for very long."

Let's hope so!

17th December 1943
The Consultation Council has decided to consign Sicily, Sardinia, and central Italy to the government of Badoglio.

20th December 1943
I received a letter today; the first in a long while, from my dear parents in Switzerland, written on 3rd November. For the first time the letter is not complete. Why have the censors cut it in this way? Why does it not contain the usual message? My worries have begun to intensify. What could have happened? I do not want to become totally discouraged.

Glasgow – 25th December 1943
Christmas! This year I did not have the traditional lunch served by the officers, but I am so happy to find myself back in Scotland. I have come, not so much as a tourist, but to improve my acquaintance with Malcolm's family, who live in the outskirts of Glasgow.

On my arrival, I first went to look for Nancy, his girlfriend, who is also in the Auxiliary Territorial Service. She is aware of our correspondence and she welcomed me affectionately. This is the first time that we have met, but I was very brief because I wanted to set off to find Malcolm's family, who were expecting me. His brother and sister, who are much younger than he is, were waiting for me at the bus stop. It was easy for them to recognise me. We headed off straight to their house.

The welcome exceeded all my expectations. They were all very complimentary towards me even though they do not know me (not even Malcolm does really), and they welcomed me as if I were a part of their family! Even the married sons and daughters (it is a very large family) came along for the occasion and they sat me next to the mother at the head of the table, and served a meal that was truly scrumptious for these times.

I noticed that they are a simple family of miners in which there is no boss, therefore the welcome that they gave me seemed to be even more affectionate. They had saved the most beautiful bedroom for me, and they were almost offended when I told them that I would not be staying the night. I wanted to continue with my travels early the following morning. We had wonderful conversation that was great fun and at the end we drank a toast to Malcolm's safe return home and mine back to Italy.

With the exception of Malcolm's elderly mother, they all accompanied me back to the bus. We formed a type of procession that aroused the attention of the few passers-by. I repeated what I had already promised the mother, that I would return soon and stay for longer.

I left the following morning heading for the famous Stirling Castle, but unfortunately I found it closed. Fortunately, I can visit it tomorrow morning.

I spent the rest of the day wandering around and now I am in a hostel on the point of retiring for the night. Tomorrow I shall go to Nancy's house before going to catch my train southbound.

London — 31st December 1943
My leave will come to an end tomorrow morning but, for now, I am a guest of the owner of the lodgings where I stayed for

some considerable time. I shall wait up with her and the other guests until midnight.

I have spent the last few days at Canterbury in the company of another comrade. I visited the city and the cathedral, then I went on as far as the coast where, for the first time, I saw the sad effects of the barrage from France; houses that had been shelled with some destruction, but nothing in comparison to the devastation caused by the bombs! I discovered that here too some of the anti-aircraft batteries are manoeuvred by comrades, quite naturally British ones.

I still have not had any news from my parents, but I have been told that the communications from Italy are interrupted even now. No matter how much I understand about the situation, I still cannot help worrying that the last message that I received from them was last June.

Even though the entire year did not bring with it any change to my situation, I still do not intend to give up hope for the future, and for myself. Because of this, I shall face the new year, carrying on with my double lottery and hoping, above all else, that it will bring the peace so desperately longed for to the whole world.

1944

From an Orderly to a Secretary

London — 1st January 1944
Today I returned to my luxurious lodgings where, to my surprise, I found a good twenty-one letters and cards, mostly from ex-roommates, sending Christmas greetings to me; evidently I did not leave them with too bad a memory of me!

No work was scheduled for today, and in the afternoon a large number of officers, of both sexes, went to the theatre to see a pantomime; a traditional part of the way of life of this country. It was great fun for both old and young!

11th January 1944
What is happening in Italy? The shootings at Ciano and Bono have left me absolutely disgusted! I shall try to find out some details. Fortunately there is a radio in the officers' lounge and when they are not in the room and I have nothing urgent to do, I rush in there to listen to it.

15th January 1944
The Allies are preparing themselves now for a landing on the coast at Lazio. When will this be confirmed?

21st January 1944
At last! Today without doubt has been a memorable date in this war. Thirty-six thousand men and three thousand transport vehicles have arrived at Anzio. My mind has not had a moment's rest since I found out. Anzio is not very far away from Rome. When will the Allies get there?

30th January 1944
There is no need to say that now, more than ever, I listen to the radio or read newspapers. I was pleased to hear today that an American division with armed vehicles has landed at Anzio and has accomplished the first major attack against the Germans, who are known to have an enormous force of infantry.

7th February 1944
Win, the girl that I share my room with, has become a friend and whenever we have the opportunity, which is quite often, we go out together to the theatre or the cinema.

Whenever I go out on my own, I visit my Italian friends,

included among whom are two families from Rome. Their husbands have been released from internment camps. They too are thrilled about the latest news, which has become the only topic of conversation.

15th February 1944
Unfortunately, the Germans continue to arrive, most of all at Cassino, where there is strong resistance. At Anzio they have tried to push the Allies out, but fortunately they have not succeeded.

20th February 1944
Being free earlier than usual, I dashed off into the centre of town to do a little shopping. Up until now I have heard people saying, "It's a small world," but I was never convinced. I changed my mind today.

As I returned, on the crowded underground — it was peak time — I saw, a short distance away, a face that I recognised. No! I thought that I must be mistaken; it surely could not be the young Polish medical student who had become, with many others, a refugee in Italy following the anti-Semitic campaign and a friend of the family. But yes, it was really he! We exchanged glances and moved towards each other, smiling.

"You are here too?" he asked, equally surprised. Then, noticing my uniform, he added, "How do you like it? Have you had any news from your parents?"

Because of the crowds, I answered with some difficulty.

"I have to get off at the next stop," he said, "but here is my address and telephone number. I'm a medic at Middlesex Hospital. We shall see each other again, shall we?"

"By all means," I answered as he was getting off the train.

I was very happy to have seen him and to know that he has graduated. I thought then, and I still do, that it really is true that the world is a small place!

25th February 1944
Here in London, I have a number of friends! I feel really happy because they are a strong support for me. The fact is that being in London is certainly pleasant, but my job is not, and so my friends help me to tolerate it all.

Now I am more or less used to the work and I do it automatically. The girls are kind and they are not boring, but after the last three years my dull life is starting to become really heavy going. How I wish that I could get rid of this rank!

3rd March 1944
This morning I had a great surprise. The Commander called me in to tell me that, on the sixth of this month, I have to go to the officer who has responsibility for the London area. I feel that it is hard to believe.

6th March 1944
Here I am back at the site. The meeting lasted from 14:30 until about 15:00. The officer was very courteous. He was aware of my situation and of all the attempts that I have made to change it. I briefly repeated details about my study qualifications and told him that my great wish now is to return to Italy. He promised that he would do everything in his power to help me to change my job but said that he will not be able to do anything to help me to transfer to Italy. Did this meeting have any purpose?

10th March 1944
Without thinking any more about the interview with the officer, with great enthusiasm, I went to collect the pass for my next leave.

Lincoln — 10th March 1944
This time I decided not to go too far away, but instead to visit somewhere that is both agricultural and industrial at the same time, and which has artistic attractions.

Yesterday I went back to Nottingham, a place that I have pleasant memories of. I went around the remains of the Norman castle and visited both the museum and the cathedral. After taking refreshments, I went for a beautiful walk along the River Trent. This morning I had to bite back my disappointment because I really wanted to see the oak tree in Sherwood Forest that is said to have housed Robin Hood. Unfortunately I did not manage to do that, but I am content enough to know that I was close to it.

Lincoln is one of the most important of the Roman cities in Britain; the cathedral dates back to the eleventh century and is widely considered to be the most beautiful in England. I climbed up to the top of the central tower from which I could see not only the port, but also its extensive hinterland.

Scarborough – 14th March 1944
From Lincoln, I carried on with my travels northwards and arrived at Hull. As this is the third major port in Great Britain, it has obviously been subjected to attack by the Germans. The destruction left me overwhelmed to the point where I wanted to leave straight away. Instead, I came to this town that has Roman origins. Apart from being a commercial trading centre with the Scandinavian countries, it is a place where people from the surrounding villages come for their holidays.

After I had found my lodgings, I went to the seaside. It helped me to forget the gloom. How different it is from "my" Mediterranean! All things considered, I think that I shall only stay here a couple of days and then start to head back.

London – 17th March 1944
Here I am again doing the same monotonous job! Every time I take a leave, I hardly ever hear about what is happening in the war. I went immediately to catch up with the news, and learnt that the Allies have accepted the programme, put together at a congress in Brindisi, for the six Italian parties to form a new government. What will the consequences be?

In the meantime, Vesuvius has woken up with a great eruption that, thank God, has not claimed any victims or caused any damage. Cassino is under attack; there is a lot of activity everywhere, but none for me!

23rd March 1944
At long last, after many months, I have received the usual message from my parents: *"All is well"*.

This good news not only comforts me, but it also helps me to bear this unpleasant situation in which I am vegetating. One day, which I hope will not be too far away, it will end!

1st April 1944
This morning, during breakfast for the officers, something funny happened to me. I have to wait on them, and to save me from having to return to the kitchen twice, I carried two teapots into the room; one in each hand. I was pouring the tea into the colonel's cup very carefully with my right hand without paying any attention to the other teapot that I was holding in my left hand.

All of a sudden I heard the major, who was sitting on the colonel's left, exclaim: "I can feel heat on my neck!"

I looked down and realised that I had poured the tea down his collar. He did not get angry with me at all; actually, he began to laugh and hurried off to get himself changed.

His batman was angry with me and came towards me exclaiming, "I had to get up early this morning to clean and iron his uniform!"

I was worried that I might be punished, but the accident was not mentioned after that, though I shall definitely remember to carry only one teapot at a time in the future!

12th April 1944
King Vittorio Emmanuele III has handed the throne over to Prince Umberto. Will there now be a change in the conditions in Italy? At every item of "important" news, I always ask myself this question in the hope that it will bring improvements and accelerate the end of the war.

15th April 1944
A few weeks have passed already since the Allies began a series of bombing raids on Germany's industries. The raids continue almost every day, even though at times, sadly, not all of the Allied aeroplanes return to their bases.

Without doubt, the German Air Force is shrinking; we hope that the same will happen to the ground forces too!

24th April 1944
Last night, I again saw H.F., the Polish medic that I met on the underground. We dined together in the city centre and I had the opportunity to ask him about his life in much more detail; it is far sadder than mine. After all that has happened to him,

he is still in good spirits, which has set a good example for me to follow. He really has made me stronger than I was.

We parted with the promise that we shall keep in contact and see each other again soon. I do hope so because he has provided the stimulation necessary for me not to get too discouraged and to carry on.

30th April 1944
After my dinner with H.F., I feel much better and calmer, and at every chance that I get, I go to see a cheerful film either with Win or on my own. I have started to laugh again, something that I have not done in months, actually in years; my future seems to be less bleak now...Is this a sign of something good?

11th April 1944
Today, the Allies have started a major offensive in Italy and they have reported much success.

15th May 1944
As the number of requests that I have put in to my superiors, and the interviews that followed them to try to make it possible for me to change jobs, have been unsuccessful, I have written a long letter today to I.T., a Member of Parliament who devotes time to Italians and does everything possible to help them. I presented my own case, asking if it is at all possible for him to do something to help me too. Will it make any difference?

8th May 1944
News from Italy; the Allies have passed Abbazia of Montecassino and today they have entered Cassino.

5th June 1944
I have not written anything in these last weeks because I have been too excited. I knew that something extraordinary was about to happen but today my suspicions became fact; the Allies have landed in Normandy. Four thousand ships and all types of little boats, and eleven thousand aeroplanes have taken part. What fantastic news! And, as if this was not enough, today the Allies have entered Rome! I am so emotional that I cannot possibly write any more!!

14th June 1944
It is now a week since "D-day". Yesterday the Germans, probably to try to assert themselves after all their defeats, launched V-1 bombs on London and these have caused the deaths of six people. However, they did not surprise the Royal Air Force; they were waiting for something of the sort to happen.

21st June 1944
From the 13th onwards, every day and every night, the V-1 bombs have fallen here in the south and, we have become quite used to the sound of the sirens. Fortunately, a large proportion of the population has been evacuated and there are innumerable refugees who have had time to get over it all.

I need hardly say that the Royal Air Force have tried their very best to defend this city from the destruction caused by the missiles that keep landing. We try not to worry too much, and our lives continue as normal. Naturally, we go into the city centre less often and when we do, without exception, we need to have a special permit.

4th July 1944
I should have been on another leave but, uncertain of where to go, I thought about visiting Malcolm's family, as I had promised. Regrettably, they could not host me, though I do not know the reason, and they asked me if I could go instead at the beginning of August. I willingly accepted!

13th July 1944
This morning, the Commander sent for me to tell me that the Ministry of War have sent him certain sections of the letter that I had sent to the Right Honourable I.T. He had obviously dealt with my letter immediately.

The Commander added straight away that I should not have done it, because all the applications have to pass through the hands of the military, and I should remember this if I am to send others in the future. Fortunately, I was not punished! I told him that I had tried to do something myself, as my commanders had not managed to get any result.

Now, this attempt has failed too! Tomorrow, I shall write another letter to the Right Honourable I.T., to thank him and to tell him the result of my attempts.

The British troops have already occupied Arezzo, and now the American troops have arrived at Leghorn, the town where my sister Elda and her family live. I do not think that she will be there any more.

In less than two months, the Allies have travelled 400km!

20th July 1944
A second attempt has been made against Hitler's life; unfortunately they did not succeed this time either! In any case, the situation would not have changed. I am certain that Hitler himself, knowing that this is a possibility, will have taken all the necessary measures.

28th July 1944
The V-1 remains the main topic of our conversation and every day we find out where the missiles have fallen and if there are any victims. Unfortunately, many parts of London have been hit, but thanks to the defence measures taken by the Royal Air Force, the numbers of deaths and wounded are relatively low.

Glasgow – 2nd August 1944
Here I am at Glasgow again. I really did not think that I would come back here, but life is full of the unexpected! Something unexpected struck me when I received the letter from Malcolm, and I shall be an unexpected guest when I arrive to pay a visit to Malcolm's family.

Because I did not want to arrive there tired, I decided to spend a day here; it is not only a port, already hit by German bombs, but also a city that is filled with art and culture. I went to visit the cathedral, which is much smaller than many others; its construction began in the twelfth century. After I had been for a good walk in one of the many parks, I went into an art gallery and then ended the day wandering around the town beginning at George Square, which is in front of the town hall. On top of a high column there is a statue of the great Scottish writer, Walter Scott.

Ayr – 8th August 1944
I arrived in this town after four unforgettable days. I really do

not think that when Malcolm returns home he will be welcomed back any more affectionately than I was. Not only his mother, but also his brother and two sisters were all competing to fill me with kindness, offering me cakes of every kind and being my guides on short walks.

In this way, I have got to know much more about their lives, which are as hard as those of any of the miners in the area. I did not hear one word about suffering or regret; on the contrary, the serene and happy expressions of the family really struck me, and from a certain point of view they have been a lesson to me.

I came to Ayr not only to see the sea, which was not very inviting for me as the waves crashed down onto the rocks, but rather to get to know the birthplace of Robert Burns, a few kilometres from here. He is the most famous writer of Scottish dialect poems. I have read a great many of them even if I do not completely understand them all.

As I did at Stratford for Shakespeare, I went to see the cottage where he was born, the mausoleum where he was buried and then various places which he has described. In particular, I visited a bridge, near to which an elderly man began to recite the celebrated poem *Brig o' Doon*. I realised that all the Scots, wherever they are, are proud of his poetry and I heard the description of the traditional "Burns Dinner", held every 25th January, for the anniversary of his birth (1759).

To be honest, I do not want to taste the "haggis", sheep's stomach filled with ground-up parts of intestines, vegetables, oats and other things.

Satisfied with everything, I am now ready to set off for "my villa"!

London – 12th August 1944
Joyce, one of my "workers", has been transferred to be nearer to her parents' home, as her mother is gravely ill.

Now Ann has taken her place. She is totally different from Joyce, who is active, orderly, educated and, to me in particular, kind. I have already called Ann to order, but not always with a good result, and because of this, my attention is constantly being drawn to her.

Everything else is all proceeding as usual, and the V-1s continue to fall! Churchill arrived at Naples yesterday, for a long visit on different fronts, not only to see Tito but also to meet the relevant task forces.

23rd August 1944
I have been following Churchill's stay in Italy with particular interest. Because of this, I know that he has visited Cassino and the ruins at Abbazia, and Siena and the Allied troops on the banks of the River Arno, as well as Leghorn and other places. In Rome he met with Badoglio, Togliatti and all the party leaders. Today, he was received by the Pope and met with King Umberto, who is now the Commander of the Italian Armed Forces.

26th August 1944
The Allies have launched another strong attack in Italy. Will this be the decisive one that will bring liberation to the whole country, allowing me finally to go home? I am quite impatient!
   In the meantime the Allies, having landed in Normandy, have reached Paris!

28th August 1944
Churchill has left for London again after having sent another message to the Italians. Unfortunately, I have not yet been able to see the written text.

4th September 1944
I have had new discussions with a senior officer. I had to repeat my "military history" once again, and the officer listened almost without interruption. Just like all the others on previous occasions, she said that she understands my situation and will try to help me change it. I added that my greatest wish is to be transferred to Italy and I asked her if this meeting could do anything to help that aim. She did not reply to the suggestion, limiting herself to repeating that she will try to help me; to do what?
   I have no more hope left, although this new meeting has proved to me that my case has not been totally forgotten and that "something" is being done. What it is, and who is considering

my situation, I do not know...The meeting is now over.

8th September 1944
Exactly one week after the end of the bombing with the V-1s, those of the V-2s have now begun. These are much bigger and quieter than the last ones, and so they do not give people the chance to reach the shelters.

The Royal Air Force have made it known that they have begun the destruction of the locations where these V-2s are being manufactured.

19th September 1944
Yesterday, I celebrated my fourth birthday in the Forces very simply because, with the V-2 bombings, we go into London less frequently. The sergeant, Win, another two girls and myself, had a drink together in a nearby bar, toasting more to an end to this war and our return to our families, than to my health.

I really do think that this will be my last birthday in Great Britain.

24th September 1944
I was not wrong in my judgment of Ann; I was proved right yesterday when she suddenly disappeared. The Commander was not very surprised either, and asked all her close companions whether they could find anything out about her disappearance. The only unpleasant consequence for the other girls is that they have to do more work.

3rd October 1944
After many months, I have received a letter from Malcolm today. He does not mention my transfer at all. I conclude from this that he too could not do anything to help my situation. However he writes, "I have good news for you. In about fifteen days' time I shall be going to see your sister. You can be certain that I shall write to you to let you know how she and her family are doing."
I am very happy, and I really do hope that he will be able to do that, though I have many doubts.

13th October 1944
During my military life, I have done many different jobs, but

never that of the police; now I have done that too! Ann's absconding did not last very long. She was found in Birmingham and I was given the job, together with one of my auxiliaries, of going to get her. We left yesterday morning, with the documents, handcuffs and the relevant instructions. We found her in a little bedroom in the suburbs of that town.

As it is not the same town as where her parents live, I do not know why she went there, or exactly where we found her. The meeting with the Commander had been very brief as we had instructions to return the same evening. Ann absolutely refused to speak to us. She only said that she was returning to work against her will.

As punishment from the Commander, she received three weeks of having her pay suspended and was prohibited from leaving the camp in her free time. I have been given the chore of keeping her under close surveillance.

22nd October 1944
Yesterday evening, I went to find an Italian friend who lives in one of the central zones. Her husband has been imprisoned on the Isle of Man and their two children have been evacuated along with the school, and therefore she is now on her own. Since the start of the V-1 bombings, she has often gone to a large shelter near to her house. She has made many new acquaintances, and she manages to pass her time quite quickly with chatting and knitting. She misses her family and this way of life is getting her down. She was very pleased to see me, and asked me to return again soon, but she does understand that now with the V-2 bombing, London has become very dangerous. In fact on a Saturday evening, I saw fewer people around than usual. How much longer will all this last?

31st October 1944
The month has ended, but I still have not received the promised letter from Malcolm. What a disappointment...

3rd November 1944
My disappointment has soon passed, as this morning I received the long-awaited letter from Malcolm. He arrived in Tuscany a little later than he had hoped but, in recompense, he managed

to find Elda, my sister, and also my parents who have gone to live with her, not at Leghorn but now at Lucca. He does not provide me with very much detail, but I can appreciate that it was not very easy and that he returned twice. He has written that everybody is doing well and this means a lot to me. He also gave me their address.

6th November 1944
There has been some compensation for the long silence because, apart from the letter from Malcolm, this morning I also received a letter from the Red Cross. Contrary to the previous one, it was written by Andrea, my brother-in-law, by hand. His handwriting aroused great emotion, as this is the first time in years (I do not remember exactly how many) I have not received a typed letter!

14th November 1944
This morning, unfortunately, the letter that I had sent direct to my family was returned to me, with the stamped message: *"There is no service; return to sender"*. It is obviously still too soon for me to expect a normal postal service, but I'll try again in a few weeks' time.

20th November 1944
I still do not believe that it actually is true! This morning the Commander sent for me. "What does she want?" I asked myself. I did not have the faintest idea.
"I have some good news for you. You have become an auxiliary again and you are to be transferred to the School for Artillerymen at Larkhill. You will be leaving us next Monday, the 27th."
"It isn't a mistake?" I asked, remembering the news of my last transfer.
"No, it really is going to happen. Are you pleased?"
"I am happy, but I should be even happier if my transfer was to Italy," I added.
Having said goodbye, I went immediately to tell Win, followed by my sergeant and then the girls. They all tell me that they are pleased for me but that they will be sad to see me leave.

However, it is true that something is actually happening! My military career has certainly not been brilliant, but that does not mean anything to me. I repeat, I really am quite happy. All of my "protests" in the form of interviews, letters and so forth, have finally served a purpose. But why has it taken so long? "Better late then never" says the proverb.

"Larkhill. Where is that?" I asked the sergeant.

"Near to Salisbury, in Wiltshire. Not too far away from London, but still too great a distance to go and come back by hitchhiking in one day."

What a pity! I have now been here exactly eleven months and I shall not be sad to leave, especially now with the danger of the V-2 bombings. It will also mean that I shall get to know another part of this country. How much more time is left? I do hope that it will not be too long!

24th November 1944

This morning I received a letter from the officer who has taken a particular interest in me. It made me very happy. It says: *"I have heard about your transfer to Larkhill. It really has been quite a difficult affair, but it will have all been well worth while if you are now to be transferred to a place where you will be happy. Let me know if the job is the one that you want. If ever a person deserves to get there, it's you. Your perseverance deserves that reward. I shall always be pleased to see you again. My best wishes for your job."*

Larkhill — 28th November 1944

Here I am at Larkhill! There was a surprise waiting for me at Salisbury Station; a van driven by a girl who had come to pick me up. Because of that, I did not have to do any searching around, and I was taken right up to the entrance of the hut where I shall be sleeping.

I left my luggage and went to meet my new Commander, who greeted me kindly. She is a young lieutenant who gave me details straight away about my new job. Alas, not only do I not like it, but also I do not know if I can do it because it involves accountancy; however I am pleased to be amongst well-educated, kind roommates who, like the Commander, welcomed me very cordially.

The camp is situated on a large flat plain that has quite

obviously been adapted for the artillerymen's exercises. The "female" sector is to be found some distance away from the "male" one, and so I have reached the conclusion that I shall rarely see my male colleagues, but then that is not really important for me anyway. There are in all about forty of us "secretaries", and we sleep in two large huts on real beds, like the ones at Lancaster. There is a small wardrobe next to each bed and there are two changing rooms on either side of the room, with showers and toilets that function mechanically, really well.

It seems strange for me no longer to have to supervise the girls who are allocated to do the cleaning!

I have not done any real work today, but I understood that soon I shall have to. First and foremost, I shall have to do sums in sterling money; pounds, shillings and pence. It will not be very easy at all, and therefore I shall need to use all my concentration.

To my surprise I have seen that working in my "office" there are also some men dressed in civilian clothes who are older than the usual age limit for people in military service. There is one man who works on my right who has kindly offered to help me any time that I find myself in difficulty.

3rd December 1944
All that is missing here is the news. There is not a radio anywhere here and, since my arrival, I still have not been able to find a single newspaper. How are the Allies proceeding in Italy? Have they arrived at any new towns? I shall ask my colleague from the office to bring in a newspaper.

5th December 1944
My first week is over and already I am quite accustomed to the camp, my roommates, and my work, which seemed to take longer at the beginning. I am very slow at my job, because I do not want to make any errors, and I do and then redo the figures, over and over again, so as to make certain. I have asked help from the man next to me only on two occasions and then not for the mathematics, but on how to use the special forms that I have to fill in. Therefore, I am more than satisfied.

Twice a week, we have to get up half an hour earlier to have breakfast and then we go to march wearing our helmets and gas masks. It doesn't bother me at all; for someone with a sedentary job, a little movement cannot do anything but good.

18th December 1944
This afternoon, I accepted an invitation from Jean who, making use of one of the vehicles from our camp that was going to Salisbury, gave me a guided tour of the town.

To begin with, we visited that splendid monument, the cathedral, about which I had already read some information. Jean added some more; it took thirty-eight years to build and it is in the English Gothic style; about one century later they added the majestic bell tower that, at one hundred and twenty-three metres, is the tallest in England. Before we entered the cathedral, Jean told me about the poem and the writings that say that it has as many windows as there are days of the year and as many marble columns as there are hours in the year. I couldn't check to see if it was true!

We then went for a walk along the river that, like the one at Stratford, is called the Avon and runs calmly, in harmony with the area, alongside the cathedral. We went along several streets in the town centre that have beautiful medieval buildings; we then hurried to get a cup of tea, not wanting to miss the return journey of the vehicle in which we came.

I returned to the camp very satisfied. I like Salisbury very much because it is ancient and tranquil and I felt very relaxed knowing that tomorrow I am due to start my new job. What I do not like, however, is that they have changed my title of "orderly", which I have had for the past three and a half years.

The problem still remains of my return to Italy. I intend to start my struggle again, which will go on until I win.

In the meantime, I have learnt that the Allies in Italy have recently done only limited fighting because they are reorganising themselves at the moment ready to begin the attacks once again, as soon as the weather improves.

15th December 1944
Today I had another special meeting; I spoke to an Italian prisoner, dressed as usual all in brown, who, being a junior officer, is the leader of a group of prisoners in a camp that is

under surveillance by the school of artillerymen. He immediately invited me to go to visit him, as he is only a few kilometres away from here. The camp is situated on a busy road and so there should not be any problems with transport. His name is Tonio M., and he asked me my first name and surname.

Shall I be able to visit his camp? Are they permitted to receive visitors? I will try to get more information.

17th December 1944
I read in the newspaper today, with unbounded pleasure, news that electrified me; some of the auxiliaries of the Auxiliary Territorial Army have already arrived in Italy, where they are helping their comrades with different chores. I quickly thought, 'If they can go, then so can I.'

I wanted to speak to the Commander to ask her to enquire about it but, unfortunately, she let me know that she is very busy at this time because Christmas is on the way. I shall have to wait for a meeting with her until after the festive period...

The days of waiting are dragging for me, but what can I do? Nothing, except try to have patience as the British have; as I've already said, they have it in their blood!

19th December 1944
It was a great surprise this morning to receive a letter from Tonio M., who writes: *"It is impossible for me to describe my emotions when I shook your hand and heard our sweet language. For one of us, enforced exiles from our native land, you cannot imagine the emotions on seeing a compatriot. You have suffered and, like you, so have I, but if until yesterday we were only strangers in this foreign ground, today we have come together. You will be the sweet, affectionate sister for me that will give my soul the strength needed during the days of waiting. Perhaps I am asking too much. Is that true? For my part, if you like, I shall continue to write to you, and if my words are a comfort for you, will you consider me to be a brother, an affectionate brother, the brother of an adventure."*

21st December 1944
Apart from sending greetings cards to friends in different parts

of the country, I sent one to Tonio to thank him for his warm letter and to tell him that I shall pay him a visit.

26th December 1944
Christmas Day was celebrated as it is in the other camps. As is the custom, a cup of tea when we woke in the morning was served to us by the officers; as was lunch. In the afternoon I went for a brief walk with a roommate who, unlike the majority, did not go home on leave.

1945
Return to Italy

2nd January 1945
Here we are in the new year! Will this be the one in which I return to Italy? I really do hope so, because I should like to be able to say that the war is finally over; this for me would signal that I shall be able to carry out my hope of being able to embrace, once again, all the people who are close to me. When will it become a reality? Can I start counting the days that are left until that marvellous moment? I think that it will better for me to wait and see what happens.

The holidays have come to an end and so I went to see the Commander, armed with a great many newspapers, and asked her to find out in detail what formalities are necessary for me to be transferred to Italy. She promised that she will give me her full support and said that she hoped that she will be able to give me some good news as early as possible.

Contrary to how I have felt in the past, I am now full of trust and I am going to begin this year with high expectations.

6th January 1945
Because I could not get hold of the information that I wanted, I went to see Tonio this afternoon. I had already alerted him to my visit, and all was well.

I found the camp easily because it is only a short distance away from the main road. The welcome that I received from him and his friends was really exceptional. I felt like a princess visiting her people...Words and actions were really indescribable! They offered me some tea which, given the circumstances, was very lavish, with all kinds of cakes and biscuits. In return I gave them a small package containing cakes and soap, but I found out that they have enough.

Tonio took me into the supplies store. I really could not believe my eyes to see such enormous quantities and so many varieties of food; spaghetti, macaroni, even salami; tinned tomatoes, coffee, sugar and so forth. So many of God's good provisions! I let him know that he is probably better off than most Italians in Italy, and he said that it was quite possible.

While drinking tea, Tonio told me that he was previously a prisoner of the Eighth Army in Libya and because of this he was now out of this "crazy war" (as he put it). After being held in two camps in Libya, he was transferred here, together with his friends, over a year ago. He has no grounds for complaint but, like me, he does not want anything more than to be able to return to his family.

When it came to my turn, I spoke about my experiences, and in this way, between chatting and nibbling at the food, the time really did fly by. Everyone asked me to return and visit again, and I do hope that I shall have the opportunity to do so.

17th January 1945
The new fighting in Italy still has not begun. It has already been quite a while since they started the bombings in Germany and yesterday it was Dresden's turn, where they have struck hard for the second time.

The Americans have been making progress on all fronts in the Far East and also in Europe. The Soviet Union began a great assault last Tuesday. Is it the spontaneous conflict that is beginning to show?

21st January 1945
I sent another letter to my parents today. It is the third. Shall I be lucky this time?

28th January 1945
I do not quite know what is happening to me; my "passion for movement" has lessened, perhaps because my thoughts are constantly upon my return voyage to Italy. How shall I travel; by land, by sea, or by air? I am quite inquisitive, but the form of transport, naturally, is not important. When will it all take place?

Because of this, I voluntarily accepted an invitation from Sylvia to go to spend this weekend with her and her parents, who do not live very far away from here.

For people who do not know me, they welcomed me very cordially and this brief break, in a family atmosphere, did me good.

6th February 1945
The emotions that I felt today are even stronger than those that I felt at the beginning of November, when I received the message written by my brother-in-law. It was a very brief letter, although

a letter is a letter, from my father! I found it hard to believe when I saw it and recognised the handwriting. I never thought that he would send one to me. If his letter has arrived here, why have mine not reached Lucca and been returned to me instead? Other than the usual sentence to say that everybody is doing well, my father wrote that he hopes to be able to return to Genoa soon, where he and my mother will wait impatiently for me. I shall write back now with the hope that we can now start a more or less regular correspondence.

18th February 1945
Yesterday, Sunday, we went out on an excursion organised by the Commander. We were accompanied by an officer who was our guide for our visit to the most famous ancient monument in Great Britain; Stonehenge, about fifteen kilometres from here.

It's strange, but I had not noticed before that all the comrades have their emblem on their left sleeve, and this morning I asked them why.

Stonehenge goes back to the Stone Age, having been built in three successive stages. The remains still stand of a great circle of about thirty stone columns, six or seven metres high. Two upright stones are crossed by one horizontal one so that they take the shape of a horseshoe. In the centre there are other columns, which have obviously fallen down. It is believed that this was an important religious site, with its centre facing towards the rising sun, and up until the beginning of the war, on the 21st June of every year, young people would gather here to celebrate the longest day of the year.

If I had not come to this camp, perhaps I would never have seen Stonehenge. I am truly happy!

28th February 1945
Another month has gone by and I still have not heard any news. I went back to the Commander who, as I had imagined, could not tell me anything new. She advised me to write a request that she will pass on. She well understands my mood and she too urged me to be patient. So as not to end our very brief conversation on this note, I asked her by what means of transport I would be returning. She answered that she was not certain, but that she thought that I shall travel by sea. As I

certainly shall not be the only one leaving, it will be necessary to find a boat that is a troop carrier.

Now I know something else. Quite frankly, I like the idea of travelling by sea.

1st March 1945
This morning I made the nth request for my transfer to Italy. Will anyone read it? Will it seriously be taken into consideration, and will it bring the desired result? In truth, after all the failures up to now, I have low expectations, but I really do not want to be pessimistic, as I usually am.

8th March 1945
This is the most advantageous camp to be in from every point of view. I am beginning, however, to feel the monotony, most probably as a result of my work, not in the same way as all those who have had the opportunity to leave London and have done so. I am also feeling nostalgic and want to go back to see my friends.

I have written to Win requesting her to ask the Commander in my name if I may go and sleep in London for a week, and to let me know the reply as soon as possible.

London – 16th March 1945
As I had hoped, I received a positive reply from Win. I asked permission to take leave, and set off immediately. What a difference it was to arrive at Spedan Tower not as one of the workers, but as a guest! Everyone was pleased to see me again, and the chatting began...

Larkhill – 25th March 1945
I have arrived back after spending a very pleasant, busy week. I had permission to go into the centre every day; when I was on my own, I went to visit my Italian friends, but whilst I was with Win, we went together to the cinema and theatre.

The sirens forced me to rush to a shelter on three occasions, but fortunately only for a brief period each time.

I felt that I needed this diversion because I returned to the camp revived and ready to wait (providing that it is not for too long!).

14th April 1945
The long-awaited day has finally arrived! The Allies have started the combat again, and everything is proceeding as planned on all fronts. I collect various newspapers, and spend all of my free time reading them.

21st April 1945
The Allies have entered Bologna, and all the other Italian cities are preparing themselves to receive them.

26th April 1945
Yesterday, I could not hold back the tears when I learnt that, even at Genoa, the Germans have surrendered. How I long to be there!

30th April 1945
One million Germans in Italy have surrendered, but that is not all; two incredible events have happened, in different places and in different ways, but with the same result; without doubt, millions of people are now filled with joy, myself included.
Mussolini has been captured, and shot when he tried to escape in Switzerland, and Hitler has committed suicide in the bunkers of the Chancellery of Berlin.
Their glory has finally come to an end in this way!

2nd May 1945
The War in Europe is over!! I can hardly believe it! I am so totally moved that I am incapable of doing anything, and I am having difficulty writing these words. For this reason I am going to stop.

16th May 1945
I needed the past two weeks to regain my composure a little; I say a "little" because all the recent events have totally confused my poor brain. Ideas, images and thoughts keep running through my mind, without taking a break. My roommates understand me, and try to calm me down with kindness. I went with them to a restaurant, to celebrate the victory and the end of the war, and hoping for my own departure.
Time is now passing too slowly for me, much too slowly...

21st May 1945
I have received a letter from Tonio. He and his friends are very happy and they hope, like me, to be able to return to Italy soon. He informed me that in a few days' time they are to be transferred to another camp, at Shaftesbury. It will be a little further away, but not too far, and I hope that he goes there soon.

31st May 1945
This historic month has now ended, but I am still here with no news about my repatriation...

14th June 1945
The weeks continue to pass slowly. Everything has become hard going for me. I have thought about taking another leave to distract me a little but I do not dare to because perhaps in my absence the long-awaited call will arrive. Am I only deluding myself?

I have a great many ideas that are constantly taking shape in my mind. One thought is that the English may have to remain in Italy for some time to "put everything in order", but those troops who have taken part in the fighting will definitely have to come home and be replaced by others. Along with these others, maybe I'll be able to go...My mind has not had a moment's peace...

30th June 1945
Almost two more months have gone by and I am still here. I have become apathetic. I do not want to do anything, and nothing interests me. My roommates have noticed and they try to encourage me in every possible way that they can. They lend me fun books, ask me to go out with them and, if they live nearby, invite me to go to spend the weekend at their homes with their families. I accepted once, most readily, but now I refuse everything...

8th August 1945
The "Great Day" that for years I have been waiting for has finally arrived! I still cannot believe it! This morning the Commander informed me that by the twelfth, I must be at the Transit Camp

in Bristol from where, a few days later, I shall depart for Liverpool, to be ready for boarding. She also is delighted for me.

I have therefore won my long and obstinate battle! As usual, even this time, I have managed to get what I desire! Naturally I am very excited. I have already invited my roommates to celebrate the victory that is now exclusively and completely mine!

11th August 1945
It is my last evening at Larkhill. My sack is almost ready. Unfortunately not all of my eight months of residence here have been happy; not because of the work this time, but because these past four years have really been so weighty for me that they have cut a great wound in my spirit...it could not be otherwise.

Now, fortunately, I am fighting back against this with a period of elation. Will this make me forget the struggle that I have been through, and all the disappointments? I do hope so.

Today, the Commander, the officers, my civil colleagues from the office, together with a great number of comrades, all bade me farewell. They asked me to let them know how everything is when I am reunited with my family, and to tell them what military life is like in Italy. I promised to write to somebody who could then pass on all my news.

I wrote a few lines to Tonio to say that I am sorry not to have seen him again.

Bristol — 14th August 1945
As I expected, I slept very little during my last night at Larkhill; I looked at the clock almost every hour and, from one o'clock onwards, I tried to imagine what was about to happen.

Although departure is at 10:48, I got up at sunrise and, after a hurried shower that took only a few minutes, I packed my last belongings, apart from my cup and cutlery that I still needed. Holding these in my hand, I went to have breakfast. I was on my own for the first time, and had to wait a short time until everything was ready. Because I was nervous, I ate quite slowly and chatted constantly with the other comrades, who arrived one after the other. I then went to the platoon office where I was given my train ticket.

I was the only person that was leaving from this camp, and the Commander, as on my arrival, kindly organised a vehicle to take me to the station. Sylvia and Jean were given permission to accompany me; their farewell hugs really moved me.

My journey was short and, even here, on arrival I found a comrade had come to collect me, as the camp is a little distance out of town.

I am now in Bristol, where I have been for the past two days. I immediately went to find information about my departure. Unfortunately, it has not yet been listed.

I hope that my stay will not be for long as it is not very pleasant here. There are only a few of us, and we do not have anything to do, except marching occasionally, and listening to briefings.

18th August 1945
Today, Sunday, I visited the town. Being a port it has been bombed repeatedly and I saw the extensive damage which, without doubt, has led to a great many casualties.

I went into the cathedral which, so they told me, is Norman in origin, but which has been altered and enlarged on several different occasions. Unfortunately, I did not reach the museum as, not knowing the road, I was worried that I might arrive back too late.

31st August 1945
I am beginning to doubt whether I shall ever embark! I went to ask on different occasions to make certain, and they have assured me that I shall be leaving this camp to go to Liverpool, not back to Larkhill as I fear. When will that happen?

I have got to know some of my roommates who have asked to go to the Middle East, and so I doubt that we shall be travelling together. Who will leave first?

5th September 1945
I discovered, with great pleasure, that there is a relatively large library here in this camp; reading, obviously, is a good way to occupy time. I have made great use of it, something that I have not done in years! I was also pleased to have found a book on the history of this town and, having particular interests, I read

about an important event that I had forgotten. It was from Bristol that *Giovanni* and *Sebastiano Caboto* departed on their two great voyages in 1497 and 1549. Bristol is therefore linked with Italy in memory of these two famous navigators.

14th September 1945
Finally, the suspense of my soul has come to an end! I have been informed that, together with some of my roommates, I shall be leaving Bristol for Liverpool at 16:00 the day after tomorrow. Now there are no obstacles in the way of my return to Italy!

I have an endless list of questions that run through my mind. How long will the journey take? Where shall I disembark, at Genoa? At Leghorn? Shall I be able to go straight away to see my parents?

17th September 1945
(On board the *"Arundel Castle"*)
I still find it hard to believe that I am really on board a steamship called the *"Arundel Castle"* that is heading for Italy!

I arrived at Liverpool at about midnight last night with a group of twenty-one auxiliaries (I had to supervise them all the time during the trip!); junior officers, and twenty-six officers among whom, to my surprise, I saw one officer from Wrexham and the comrades that I got to know at Bristol, heading for the Middle East. It will be quite a long journey for them if they have to go to Italy first! There were also a few nurses and a group of artistes who are going to entertain the troops.

A special train, very long and crowded, brought us to within a few metres of the steamship. We stopped only once, at Shrewsbury where we were offered a cup of tea that we drank most gladly.

At Liverpool, after having remained almost an hour in the passenger waiting room, where we were offered another cup of tea and were given the numbers of our cabins, we formed a line to go on board. Each one of us was given a light woollen khaki-coloured blanket. Will it be necessary in Italy?

In fifteen minutes we went to our cabins; each had sixteen bunk beds. We deposited our sacks and blankets, and went to gather in the dining room where a hot meal was waiting for us.

Although we were not very hungry — we had been given a great quantity of sandwiches at Bristol — we ate with pleasure, after which, exhausted, we went to lie down on our very comfortable beds.

This morning, I had decided that I would not get up for breakfast, which was at 08:30, but, at the last moment, I changed my mind and I am very glad that I did; we were offered fresh fruit and eggs!

Later, we were given the first instructions for our journey. We have been given permission to go onto only one deck together with officers, both male and female; therefore it is goodbye to the junior officers and soldiers; there will be no fraternizing with you!

Shortly after this, I went to see this deck and found that it was already full. What a surprise I had when I realized that we were in front of a long breakwater that I had seen many times, from a distance...Many memories I have of the camp came into mind; of the people that I had met there, who had become my friends straight away. I never thought that my return journey to Italy would ever begin from here!

We were each given some sheets of paper together with three envelopes to enable us to send letters to our friends and families. I have so many that it was difficult to make a choice. I made the decision and wrote just a few lines to a friend in London, one in Liverpool and also to my roommates at Larkhill.

In the meantime I heard that we are setting off at 16:00 heading directly for Alexandria in Egypt and then moving on to Naples. It is going to be us, therefore, that will have the longer journey and not, as I believed, the comrades who are heading for the Middle East. Unfortunately, my meeting with my parents will have to be delayed by a few days but, in compensation, I shall be happy to see the country where I grew up and, if it is possible, my relatives who still reside there.

Instead of 16:00, we left our mooring at 18:00. Together with everyone else, I watched the last operations to cast off. After a few minutes the anchor disappeared. Farewell Liverpool! Shall I ever see you again? My thoughts turned reminiscently to my arrival at Folkestone and then at London.

Six years have passed; six difficult years, filled with uncertainty, anxiety, fear and disillusionment, but I have also experienced a great many things and have learnt so much; firstly, to be patient!

Dinner began at 19: 30. What a pleasure it was to be served. I feel as if I have become an officer!

18th September 1945

It is my birthday today! As soon as I woke up, I realised that we were rolling. The sea was far from calm but, nevertheless, I felt well and had a great appetite, unlike virtually all my roommates, who remained in their beds. I had a shower in a hurry, and rushed off to the breakfast table where there was a plentiful meal waiting for me.

Last night I had told Ethel, who sleeps above me, that today is my birthday and this morning I realised that she had spread the news because I received a large number of congratulations, even one from the officer from Wrexham, who gave me a small, highly-perfumed tablet of soap!

At eleven o'clock, on the deck, we were each assigned a jacket that is to be used in the case of emergencies, and the number of our seat in the life-saving longboats. At 16:00 they carried out the relevant checks.

In the meantime, we made new acquaintances. Vivian and I have got to know three officers from the Dutch Merchant Navy who, trapped in their country, hid from capture by the Germans and joined the Resistance movement. They are now going to disembark in Italy to relieve their colleagues, who have been out there for the duration of the war.

As we chatted away, time flew by and, after dinner, we continued to talk until 22:15. Even here, a type of discipline is enforced, and at 22:30 there is a check to make certain that we have all retired for the night.

19th September 1945

It is true that we are no longer in a camp but we are still members of the Auxiliary Territorial Service! Therefore, this morning, we were informed of the programme for the day. From 09:30 until 10:00 gymnastics; from 11:00 until 11:30 exercises relating to what to do in case of emergency; from 17:00 until 17:30 attendance at a briefing. Today, the briefing was held by a major, who is a medic, on the subject of the most common illnesses in the Middle East and the precautions that we must take in order to avoid them.

We are left with many hours of free time and I pass many of them contemplating my great friend, the sea, which still holds a deep fascination for me, or else chatting with one of the Dutch officers, named Fred.

Today, the weather has not been so good. It rained this afternoon and so I was forced to take shelter in one of the halls together with some other comrades. Shortly afterwards, Fred came to tell us that we could see a part of the Spanish coast. We hurried to take a look, and we caught a glimpse of Cape Finisterre. In spite of the fact that we have been at sea now for three days, we were all very excited. I realise what it must have been like for Colombus, when he saw land again after two months!

A few minutes later, we were cut off once again, seeing only the sea and the sky. In all honesty, we are not completely isolated as we do have a radio on board that receives the BBC News three times a day; at 08:30, 12:30 and 18:00. It was through this means that I heard that the vice-head of the Italian Government had arrived in London to take part in a conference on the partitioning of Trieste and Istria.

It is now 22:00; the weather has improved; the sea is calm and the clouds have disappeared. Tomorrow, we shall have a splendid day.

20th September 1945
This morning, after breakfast, the sergeant major ordered us to polish our buttons. After all this time, it is no longer possible to see the coat of arms upon them. However, when we had finished our gymnastics, the officers took off their jackets and we were given permission to do the same. All the "shining" therefore has been for nothing!

At 11:40, having passed Cape Saint Vincent, we entered "my" Mediterranean. I felt so emotional when I saw it again after so many years! I waved to it in my mind, just as if I were seeing an old friend.

21st September 1945
The temperatures have soared and this has upset many of the others, but not me! Life on board has taken on another facet;

instead of being a military transport ship, it seems to have turned into a cruise ship. The clothes that the officers, of both sexes, are wearing are almost civilian ones, with T-shirts and shorts of various colours.

On the bridge today, the dog races began. As is well known, I am against all games of chance, but this time I allowed myself to be tempted, and I bought three tickets that cost one shilling each. I am pleased with this pastime, because it shows an aspect of English life that I did not know about. Now I can see that the English are the same as all the others who get excited and shout as if the cardboard dogs were real. I think that the "calmness" of these people is only a fairy tale

23rd September 1945
This is the last day for us to hand in our letters to be posted. I have written a few. Will they get there?

Before dinner, by chance, I overheard a conversation between an officer and a member of the crew. They had just received an order for the Commander of the *"Arundel Castle"* to continue for Haifa, Port Said, Malta, Tolone, Naples and Bombay. What will happen? Do we all have to make these sea crossings?

Later, I found out that we must disembark at Port Said to wait for another ship, which will then take us to Naples.

My return home has begun to appear to me as a "castle in Spain"...Everything about this steamship seems to be unreal...The opportunity to spend a few days in Egypt — apart from the fact that I shall be reunited with my family a little later than expected — does not bother me.

This evening, in one of the halls I listened to some music and I watched some couples dancing, one of whom was our sergeant major with a colleague. We auxiliaries were also invited but I refused, as I have never liked dancing.

I still have not mentioned that we have left Biserta behind and the next land that we pass will be that of Pantelleria, Italy. This will be another emotional moment for me. How I should like to disembark there and to fly on to Lucca!

Frankly, however, my mind has turned to Egypt.

25th September 1945
The time is 15:30. In a couple of hours, instead of arriving at

Alexandria, we shall be arriving at Haifa. What a pity that this town is not Genoa! The change in schedule is due to the fact that the situation in Palestine has become more complicated and the troops are now needed there.

Immediately after lunch, we lined up on both sides of the deck, with a glass in our hand, to drink a toast...to whom? What for? But we all drank, with pleasure. We are all still happy.

I am scribbling these words down, as writing is not very easy...Here we are, getting closer to the port. The pilot has already got on board and the new flag is flying...The first impressions of the town were of some shining landmarks and then, slowly, I began to distinguish all the white office buildings. What a contrast it is to Liverpool, which is very dark! I can see a few masts of ships that have been sunk, almost certainly by the Italians as they took flight. Apart from that, the town does not look at all damaged. The port is full of English ships and there are others of many different nationalities...I can hear the sound of our anchors being dropped...

The formalities have started immediately; there are several motorboats with policemen aboard; I can see one wearing a Moslem tarboosh, and they are drawing closer to the *"Arundel Castle"*...There are other motorboats with Arabs aboard who have come, most probably, to collect the officers' baggage.

I have written these sentences at intervals, and now it is almost 18:00. I can see two motorboats filled with several of our comrades leaving the ship... Farewell, boys and girls, and good luck!

Haifa — 26th September 1945
In less than two hours last night, the *"Arundel Castle"* was emptied. We were informed that there was a special motorboat for us that would take us to visit the town, and bring us back to the ship at 22:00. Most of us, including the Dutch officers, did not want to lose this opportunity and, in only a few minutes, we were all aboard the motorboat. Once ashore, we separated; Fred and I headed towards one of the roads rising up to the town centre. We were pleased to see that there is no damage. We went into a small restaurant, and I was very happy to taste typical Arabic dishes after so many years.

As we went back down towards the port, we passed in front

of a jeweller's shop. Fred asked me, "Can I possibly buy you an engagement ring?"

I was left, understandably, dumbfounded because I had considered him to be another one of the usual short-term friends. When I could speak, I asked, "Is this a joke?"

"No, I'm very serious."

Walking along, we talked about endless things, first and foremost, the fact that we know so little about each other...

27th September 1945
Fred's proposal did not allow me to sleep. Are his intentions really serious? Should I believe him? On the other hand, he is no longer a boy; he is four years older than I am...I soon thought that I should go to speak to his Commander.

Port Said – 28th September 1945
This morning at about 08:00 we left Haifa, which I shall never forget. Shortly afterwards, we arrived in the town where I spent the first seven years of my life. I never imagined that I should return here under these circumstances! We were all told that we would have to disembark and wait for another ship that will take us to Italy.

I asked if I could take "leave" straight away. I have been allowed to take between one and two weeks, but I have to leave the telephone number of my aunt, in case they need to recall me sooner.

Alas, I did not know it! With the aid of a police officer, I made enquiries and I eventually managed to find it. At first I thought about phoning the number, but then I declined, as I should prefer to pay her a surprise visit.

Alexandria – 2nd October 1945
Here I am in this town, and I really do feel as though I am dreaming. At Port Said, having bid farewell to the members of the crew and to my Dutch friends who remained as the last passengers aboard, we disembarked in order to continue on our long trip to Napoli.

Fred and I exchanged addresses and parted, unhappily, and he begged me to write to him as soon as possible. I shall do that, because the information that I received from his

Commander about his behaviour is first class from every point of view. I have always been a fatalist and therefore I must wait to see what destiny will bring!

Shortly afterwards, a train arrived on a track close to the *"Arundel Castle"*. Together with our sacks and coats, we took our places. After a journey of over six hours, I got off here whilst the other seven passengers remained on board to continue their journey on to Cairo.

I caught a taxi and went immediately to see my aunt. I really cannot describe the surprise that she got; she had thought that I was already back in Italy! She telephoned her children and grandchildren, some of whom came immediately to see me. To be part of a family again, even though not directly, made me quite emotional. The chatting went on until late, and really did exhaust me.

10th October 1945
These past few days have flown by! I have borrowed some civilian clothes from one of my cousins. Wearing them, I feel more at liberty.

I sent a telegram to Lucca announcing my arrival and also to ask for my parents' address, pleading with them to let me know straight away.

My outings have almost always been kept short, just in case the military have called me to return to work; nevertheless I spent a day at the beach where, with enthusiasm, I flung myself into the sea, which was still warm...What a difference from the English sea! I also went to Cairo to visit another aunt who wanted me to stay with her for a few days. When I said that I could not, she took me to see the famous pyramids. What a joy it was for me to see those ancient monuments!

I received a telegram from Lucca yesterday, with my parents' new address; this evidently means that they could not return to the old apartment. What a pity!

My unexpected visit to Egypt has lasted longer than I had anticipated, and tomorrow I shall return to Port Said.

12th October 1945
(Aboard the *"Arundel Castle"* sailing towards Italy)
I left Alexandria with a feeling of sadness, on a train filled with

military people and civilians of mixed nationalities, though mainly Polish. There were also a great number of Italian prisoners, amongst which there were many officers, and also entire Yugoslavian families with an endless number of children, and others. All of them, like me, are returning to their homes. If the houses are no longer there, then I must do something to help to put the country back into order...When we reached Port Said we saw a huge steamship full of troops, both black and white. For a short while we believed that we should also have to get on board, but it would have been impossible, it was far too full!

The Poles had already started to board, but we were given permission to go ahead of them. The members of the crew welcomed us on board, I should say, almost affectionately. What a pleasure it was for us to see so many recognisable faces!

We were not given the same cabin again, but another one a little smaller, and, after we had deposited our baggage, we went to have lunch.

I went up on deck and then I realised that the *"Arundel Castle"* had undergone certain changes; it has been repainted and is no longer totally grey. Some sections are now red, and it has a new, merrier look.

The Italian prisoners were embarking together with a few Franciscan friars. Are they also prisoners?

For the entire afternoon, I chatted to a Swiss lady; we share some of the same friends. Once again, I realise that the world is a small place.

After dinner, we had to practise using the life jackets, and the day ended with me taking two aspirins and going to bed; spending a day like this is more than enough to give me a severe headache.

Not an hour had passed before I realised that already we were moving. I hurried to get up and get dressed, and rushed to the deck. I wanted to say goodbye to Port Said, to Egypt actually...

It is 22:30. Even though it is dark, I could still distinguish the steamships and the buildings. We passed in front of the offices of the Canal Company. I wanted to see the lighthouse, behind which is the house where we once lived. Farewell "Calascione House", the house of my carefree childhood!

Looking carefully, my eyes becoming accustomed to the dark, I could just make out the statue of Ferdinando di Lesseps who planned and completed the cutting of the Suez Canal. Goodbye, but is it *au revoir*, Egypt?

14th *October 1945*
Another two days of sailing. The weather is perfect and the sea is so calm that the ship seems to be sliding along on it. Tomorrow we arrive at Taranto and after a few more days I shall be in Lucca, from where I shall head off for Genoa. Am I dreaming? No. It really is true! I slept only a little, and I believe that it will be the same for the next few nights.

This morning at 07:00, we were told that we do not have to wear our uniform jackets from the camp again, but we can keep our trousers, and we are all satisfied.

After breakfast, we went up onto the deck and we could feel the air, noticeably, was much fresher. Our favourite pastime at the moment is chatting to people of other nationalities. There is a group of officers from New Zealand, and it gives me pleasure to learn something about their country.

Last night, I spoke to some Italian officers who have to remain on the lower deck. One of the officers is from Sassari and I was surprised when he referred to me by using *"voi"*, the formal Italian word for "you", instead of *"tu"* which is informal. Evidently he had not forgotten the past! (*This change was initiated by Mussolini in an attempt to make daily speech more courteous.*)

This morning by 07:00, I was already on the deck. To my surprise, I saw some islands and, shortly afterwards, Greece — another country to add to the list of countries that I have passed — with its Cape Matapan. My thoughts immediately went to the great naval battle in these waters, between the English and the Italian fleets, in 1941. How many victims must there have been then...and now everything is so calm and peaceful.

My mind travelled a long way back in time, and the names of writers, artists and philosophers, together with images of monuments, rapidly alternated.

I should have liked to stop, if only to see the Acropolis! It would have made a splendid follow-on from my visit to the pyramids, but I am not on a cruise and, if nothing else, I must remember my uniform!

It is now 18:30; they have just announced that early tomorrow morning we shall arrive at Taranto, where we shall disembark before lunch time...Will it really be like this? I am almost certain that tonight I shall not close my eyes.

Taranto — 15th October 1945
I have finally arrived back in Italy! I can scarcely believe it. My long struggle has finally come to an end. It now seems almost impossible that it is more than six years since my departure.

Disembarking was not so easy as it was at Port Said because the *"Arundel Castle"* was too big to enter the port and it had to drop anchor just outside. Large motorboats came to collect us and, after only a few minutes, we were standing on dry land.

How emotional it was for me, far more so than anything I have ever experienced before. Greetings, Italy! I have been longing for you ever since the moment that I left you, and now I am so happy once more that my eyes are filling with tears.

We went on foot to a hotel where we were served a good lunch. We have been told that we have to spend the night here before we set off for Naples tomorrow. Each one of us has been given our address, written in code, to transmit to our families.

This afternoon we went in a group to have a look around the town; it is one that I do not know, and in the evening I drank a glass of sherry to celebrate my return.

Naples — 17th October 1945
We only arrived here this afternoon. Most of the means of transport, especially the trains, are not running regularly yet, and they do not link the towns. From Taranto we had to go to Bari where we spent the night, and from there we came to Naples in a motor van, crossing Italy from the Adriatic Sea to the Tyrrhenian.

20th October 1945
I still have not departed, and I get the feeling that I shall not do so for quite some time yet. I have sent telegrams to Genoa and Lucca to say that I still do not know when I shall be able to get there.

Eight of us were accompanied to our lodgings where we were served a good meal prepared by Italian girls and boys who were flabbergasted to hear me speak "their" language "so well"! We were allocated beds in two rooms in a large building situated just in front of the sea on the Chiaia Riviera. I could not be any luckier!

On Friday, I asked permission to have a month's leave; just as the English military do when they arrive home after being abroad. I was granted it immediately; apart from the leave, however, I shall also need to have various permits for travelling and for lodgings. Unfortunately, the Commander does not know when I shall be able to leave because the rail service has reduced the number of stations to a minimum; my journey to Genoa will take me a very long time, since I cannot get there directly.

Naturally, I am free for the weekend and I shall be free until I depart, as I have now been assigned my new job in the office of "Claims and Employment" in Rome. I am happy; not only because I shall be in the capital, but also because I have cousins and friends who live there. "All roads lead to Rome," says the proverb and it is true for me!

All things considered, this extended stay at Taranto has not displeased me at all and I went to have a walk around the town centre on Saturday morning. While there, I found myself, by chance, in front of a maritime office. Out of curiosity, I went inside to ask them where Fred's steamship was to be found. With great surprise and pleasure, I learnt that he will be arriving right here, tomorrow! I can hardly believe it! Is it destiny, therefore, that wants to unite us?

In the office they asked me if I had a message for a member of the crew, and so I wrote a message for Fred including my address, asking him, if it is possible, to come and find me after he has finished work. Shall we really see each other again so soon? It seems impossible to me!

25th October 1945
Yes, we did meet again, and we spent two days together!
Yesterday we went to Pompeii and as we were returning, we had had to walk as far as the Torre Annunziata; it is incredible but true.
I was pleased to be able to give him my parents' new address at Genoa where he can send letters to me while I am on leave.

After these two unexpected and pleasurable days, we parted once more without knowing where or when we should see each other again...We are both certain, however, that if destiny has let us meet each other, then it will continue to help us.

Now I have to wait to leave for Genoa with no stopoff coming from the south at Lucca, as I had hoped, because there are still no trains as yet for that town. I shall have to take a detour as far as Milan and, from there I shall be able to continue to Genoa. The journey will be anything but easy, but fortunately, there are members of the military at all of the stations, who will be able to help me. When shall I arrive in "my" town?

Genoa – 30th October 1945
Since Sunday 27th, I have been here with my parents! The day that I have been dreaming about has finally arrived! We were all so overwhelmingly emotional that for a few minutes we could not even say one single word!

The journey was not as difficult as I thought it might have been mainly because the English military helped me. I was full of nervous excitement all the way from Milan to Genoa...As soon as I left the station, I caught sight of the Colombo Monument; I found it hard to believe, but then I calmed down and greeted it like a friend...

There is another family living where we previously lived, and a taxi brought me to this unknown house...It does not matter though; I am reunited with my mother and father after six years! This fact is all that counts. I found them in mediocre health.

My brother Renzo came with Maria Bianca and I was very pleased to meet him.

After that initial period of silence we began chatting, and that continued almost uninterrupted, and will almost certainly continue in this way for the rest of my stay here.

Unfortunately my immense joy was saddened by some very unfortunate news; my mother's brother, his wife, and their twenty-six-year-old daughter, have been the victims of a brutal Nazi attack and have, like many other dear friends, been sent to a concentration camp. My parents told me about their escape, with the help of Maria Bianca, from Genoa and the various stages, filled with danger, they had to make to reach Lucca.

How they have suffered! Fortunately, they miraculously managed to make the journey, and to avoid capture.

Another one of the important subjects of our chats was, naturally, Fred. It was a huge surprise for them, mainly because I have always said that I shall remain a spinster because I love my freedom…The high point of the news for them was to hear that Fred is not English but Dutch and, not only this, but also that we have been together for such a short time.

Nevertheless, I managed to convince them that I know that this will be a big step (and I hope that I shall be able to make it very soon) and that I am well aware that it will be anything but easy. That decision has been made because those few days that we spent together were enough to make me realise that Fred is a serious person and that he is the one most suitable for me.

On Monday, I went to the main depot where I claimed the rations for the whole month. It was such a large quantity that I did not quite know how to transport it. A fellow comrade understood my difficulty straight away and sent for a colleague who took me home in a jeep. There is plenty for all three of us!

My mother told me that Malcolm, of whom we have spoken so much, helped them at Lucca by transporting their rations for them.

12th November 1945

The news of my arrival has spread with the speed of lightning and an endless number of friends want to see me. I have already been to see a few of them and they treat me as if I am a heroine. I never expected this treatment!

I have also begun to write a few lines to my English friends who are waiting impatiently to know if, when, and how I arrived here.

There is so much for me to do that I must skim over this diary!

30th November 1945

As a result of the days that were lost in travelling, I asked for an extension of my leave; I was given four additional days. Tomorrow, however, will be my last day at home! Never in my life has a month passed so quickly!

In Italy, as in England, I shall be given ten days' leave every three months, but some of that will be lost because of the poor railway situation. Let us hope that that will improve soon!

Rome – 4th December 1945
I have now reached my destiny in the Italian military! My return journey, unfortunately, was worse than the incoming one. From Genoa, I ended up at Novara! And at Milan, there was no train leaving for Rome that same day.

I turned for help to a companion in the Auxiliary Territorial Service, and an officer guaranteed that there would be a train the following day and gave me permission to spend the night with a friend called Renata. I managed, with great difficulty, to get in contact with her; she took me into her arms with great joy and surprise! We chatted until well into the night.

The next morning, I presented myself in front of the same officer; but there were still no trains leaving Milan!

So as not to waste any more time, he sent me by jeep to Novara where I found a train reserved for military, going directly to Rome. The station was filled with military people and, outside it, jeeps, so it was not difficult for me to find one to take me to Piazza della Sapienza where my new offices are to be found.

I met the officers straight away; the Commander, who has the stripes of a captain, and a junior officer; both of whom were kind and courteous.

The appearance of these lodgings reminds me of Spedan Tower in London, but now, fortunately, I am no longer in those same circumstances.

I have already been given information about my new job, which will start tomorrow. I shall go to the office with two comrades; Audrey, with whom I share a bedroom, and Sylvia. A jeep is to collect us, and take us to report to work.

8th December 1945
Today is Sunday and I have had to stay in the office (mercifully we are no longer in a camp), to get my uniform organised, and to speed up some of my correspondence. I have managed to do all this with composure for the first time in many years!

I have now been in the office for three days, and even if my job were uninteresting, I should not be unhappy. I have to translate letters received from Italians who have had their property requisitioned, and who now want compensation.

The environment in which I work is really quite extraordinary; the office is situated in a beautiful square called Piazza Augusto Imperatore, the windows have views over the small square of Corso Umberto, and it occupies an enormous floor area. In my department, apart from Audrey and Sylvia, there is also a sergeant; in the other there are five girls and two Italian boys. We are all under a colonel, who is very correct and strict.

Instead of going into the offices for lunch, Audrey and I went for a long walk along the Tiber while eating a very tasty sandwich. I think that we shall do this often.

I really do not have any reason to complain! The only thing that I should like to know is how long I have to stay here.

26th December 1945

Yesterday, Christmas Day, our Commander, following the usual tradition, brought us a cup of tea in bed. For lunch the Italian girls, who obviously did not want to break with tradition, served us with an Italian-English meal with lots of turkey and vegetables, after which the flaming Christmas pudding arrived. We were all pleased and content, and ate everything.

In the afternoon, Audrey and I went to find Lara, a colleague from the office with whom I have already formed a good friendship; and in the evening, once again, we joined together to eat another excellent dinner!

1946
Fred

2nd January 1946
The new year has begun. I am in Italy, but not with my parents. I did telephone them, however, to let them know that I shall return to see them, soon. This way we felt much closer!

Tuesday evening, the last one of 1945, we all went together — with two officers and the sergeant major — to our club where there was a special variety performance followed by a dance; very pleasurable for my comrades, but not for me.

Fortunately, we only waited for the new year to begin. Shortly after one o'clock we set off back again.

Yesterday too was a free day, and today we returned to our offices where a good part of the morning was spent offering and receiving 'New Year' greetings.

15th January 1946
The days are really flying by! I have now been here for six weeks and not a single minute of that time has been monotonous. I am so busy in the office that I do not have enough time to do all the things that I should like to do, out of it!

My own correspondence has increased as I now write to Fred twice a week; not only to tell him what has happened in my day, but also to ask him about himself and his family. In this way, I shall be able to get to know them all better. He writes to me even more frequently than I do to him, almost every evening, and he posts the letters the minute that he gets into a port.

2nd February 1946
This morning I had a wonderful surprise: The Commander told me that I am allowed to take another leave, for ten days. Even by this time, I shall still need to add another four days for my journey.

I have decided to go to Lucca, if it is now possible to enter.

Lucca — 6th February 1946
I have learnt that, if I go by way of Florence, I can get to Lucca. I immediately asked for my rail ticket, and the permits necessary for me to go into the town. As soon as I received these, I telephoned Elda to tell her about my forthcoming visit, without giving her a precise time, and on Saturday morning I left for

Florence. I found an office of the Auxiliary Territorial Service there, and they took it upon themselves to help me. Shortly afterwards, they told me that I should have to go to Pisa, and from there I could get to Lucca. I did exactly that, without too much difficulty, but with a long delay.

At Pisa, I telephoned at 18:00 to say that I definitely should get there that evening but, once again, I was not able to give them the exact time. I found all three of them at the station. They had waited for me for more than two hours! There was no shortage of tears, but they were tears of joy. I am so happy to have found them all in good health and to learn that Alberto, whom I had last seen as a little boy of six years old, had now become a smart young man.

As at Genova, the majority of the days were spent chatting, and I heard some really dreadful stories about the disappearance of some dear friends from Leghorn. Naturally of course, we spoke about Malcolm, and his great kindness, and we all regret that we have not received any recent news from him.

I played the role of a tourist, walking along the town's wall and visiting the churches, museums and other places of artistic merit that I previously did not know. I enjoyed myself very much.

The "family trio" cannot wait for the time when they will be able to return to their own home at Leghorn, and they hope that this will be within another month or two.

After such a long struggle, and with a sense of pride for having achieved my objective, I am now very happy to have seen all my family once more!

Rome – 12th February 1946
Back in the office, I immediately set to work as I found a whole case of letters waiting to be translated.

It is in this way that my life continues…but for how long like this?

I should not be so preoccupied if I did not have a set idea; that of my marriage. Both Fred and I wish to marry as soon as possible. I shall therefore wait for another couple of months and then ask for a leave to enable me to return for this purpose to London. When I get there and am married, perhaps I shall be demobilized from the Army to enable me to go to my new country.

* * * * * * * *

I shall now bring this diary to an end, saying, as it is told in children's fairy tales, apart from Fred not being a prince and myself not being a princess, I hope that in Holland we shall be able to live a long and happy life.